WINDOW STYLE

WINDOW STYLE

Y V O N N E   R E E S

VNR VAN NOSTRAND REINHOLD
_____ New York

A QUARTO BOOK

Copyright © 1990 Quarto Publishing plc

Library of Congress Catalog Card Number 89-70681
ISBN 0-442-30295-9

Published in the U.S.A. by
Van Nostrand Reinhold
115 Fifth Avenue
New York, New York 10003

Distributed in Canada by
Nelson Canada
1120 Birchmount Road
Scarborough
Ontario M1K 5G4, Canada

This book was designed and produced by
Quarto Publishing plc
The Old Brewery
6 Blundell Street
London N7 9BH

Senior Editor: Susanna Clarke

Designer: Karin Skånberg

Illustrator: Sally Launder

Picture Researcher: Sheila Geraghty

Art Director: Moira Clinch
Assistant Art Director: Chloë Alexander
Editorial Director: Carolyn King

Typeset by Ampersand Typesetting (Bournemouth) Ltd
Manufactured in Hong Kong by
Regent Publishing Services Ltd
Printed by Leefung Asco Printers Ltd, Hong Kong

16 15 14 13 12 11 10 9 8 7 6 5 4 3 2 1

Library of Congress Cataloging-in-Publication Data

Rees, Yvonne.
    Window style/Yvonne Rees.
        p.   cm.
    ISBN 0-442-30295-9
    1. Windows.   2. Interior decoration.   I. Title.
NK2121.R44   1990
747'.3--dc20

CONTENTS

———◇———

Chapter One

LETTING IN LIGHT

◇

WINDOWS PAST AND PRESENT

Windows, whether large, small, glazed or shuttered, have been an integral part of our homes since the first shelters were built. Their principal functions were to provide light and air, and in the earliest dwellings they were no more than a crude hole in the wall or roof, as their original name of "wind eye" or "wind hole" suggests. Since then, windows have evolved to such a level of sophistication that we can construct complete buildings from seemingly no more than sheets of glass. In modern homes, protected from the cold (or in warmer climates the heat), they help to conserve energy, and they open wide to allow us to take full advantage of good weather. In addition to their practical advantages, windows give a house its character. More than any other architectural feature, their shape, size and number create the essential style both inside and out.

The history and development of the window is inextricably linked with climate, culture and the development of glass. The different styles which can be seen throughout the world today have grown from the practical needs of each country's inhabitants. Homes built in snowy mountainous regions have for centuries been constructed with small shuttered windows to keep out the cold. Likewise, the enclosed courtyard house of the Mediterranean and North Africa has few external windows; most of the light and ventilation is provided by larger openings arranged around an internal courtyard.

IN THE BEGINNING

The principle of placing a length of stone or wood across two uprights to form an entrance in a wall was known to the earliest civilizations. It was in this way that they built their windows – smaller versions of their doorways – to lighten their homes, public buildings and temples. Many of the great architectural works of the ancient Egyptians, the Sumerians and the Greeks still survive, and in their magnificent ruins can be seen window openings constructed with mathematical precision.

Left This fairy-tale tower with its pretty, wedding-cake windows is in fact Sintra Town Hall in Portugal.

Previous page Classic black-and-white cottage in Germany with a fine pair of large casement windows and an interesting, decorative skylight above the heavy oak front door.

Right French château with tiny slit windows intended to provide good defense rather than adequate illumination.

The simple dwelling houses of the great civilizations have, for the most part, been destroyed by time and archaeological remains are few, but it is likely that these early peoples would have used wooden shutters and cloth or skin hangings to keep out inclement weather, for although glass was known in the ancient world, it was not developed for glazing purposes.

By A.D. 120, the Roman Empire stretched across the length and breadth of Europe. Along with the palaces and temples of their great cities grew narrow, twisted streets lined with buildings not dissimilar in appearance to those of our cities today. On each side of these cobbled roads rose wood, brick and plaster houses over 60ft. (18.5m) high, built with vast bay windows to flood the dwellings with light and air. Unfortunately, they also flooded the buildings with heat, cold and drafts, as the ordinary Roman had nothing more than folding wooden shutters or animal skins to keep out the elements. However, in the richer households, the occupants were already making use of thin sheets of mica – a mineral of crystalline structure which can be split into thin, uniform, translucent sheets – or small sections of glass cast in shallow molds to fill their window openings. Panes of rough glass also filled the roofs of their bath houses, providing light while hermetically sealing in the heat.

While the great empires of the world flourished, the inhabitants of northern Europe lived in relatively primitive conditions. Their rough stone, turf or wooden houses were often built with no more than a doorway, but most had some form of small opening set just below the roof to provide a little additional light and allow the smoke from the cooking fires to escape. These openings

The Roman invasion of northern Europe made little difference to the building techniques of the indigenous populations. When the Romans left, most of their works were pulled down and the material re-used. However, gradually techniques improved, and across Europe fortified stone dwellings were built to house the rich, their thick walls giving way to tiny windows with carved stone surrounds.

By the eleventh century, stone was becoming more widely used for buildings of importance. The great Norman architects set to work on their castles and churches everywhere, and trade with neighboring countries meant that glass could be purchased from the great centers of Italy, France and Germany. Meanwhile, for the yeoman farmers and workers, conditions were improving, too. Wood was a natural building material used throughout much of northern Europe, and as methods of timber framing became more sophisticated, with heavy oak beams supporting walls of mud or clay, so windows became larger and were often divided by horizontal supports known as mullions. Timber-framed buildings naturally had wooden mullions, set between the wall plate at the top and the sill at the bottom. Likewise, stone houses had mullions made of stone, but blocks long enough to form the supporting beam, or lintel, were expensive, as they often needed to be transported from distant quarries. To keep the costs down, the mullions were made from shorter lengths of stone, resulting in small, squat windows.

Glass was made in Britain as early as the thirteenth century, but it remained an expensive luxury and was rarely used for windows, even in the best houses. Instead,

Above Windows and balconies of a Venetian palazzo, showing the influence of the East (top). Leaded, mullioned window in a Tudor house (middle). Simple wooden shutters and windowbox (bottom).

were of necessity small, as the structure of the buildings and the bitter climate made larger windows impractical. In the colder winter months, wooden shutters were lashed across the openings and the cracks stuffed with rags to keep out the wind, rain and snow.

the wealthy merchants and the aristocracy used oiled paper or fabric, or thin slices of translucent horn stiffened with a diamond pattern of latticed wood to fill the drafty openings. These were combined with heavy wooden internal shutters, which were folded across the opening from inside.

Throughout medieval times, the basic design for poorer homes remained the same. But the rich had money to spend on prestigious dwellings, and style became more important. The three-sided bay window, with its advantages of greater views and increased light was introduced into the great houses of the fourteenth century to provide extra light for the banquet hall table. At the same time, projecting bays from the upper floors – oriel windows – were built, and both styles remained fashionable into the fifteenth century when they were glazed with expensive leaded lights and decorated inside and out with vaulted ceilings, moldings and carved friezes. For the very wealthy, these grand windows were also fitted with glass panels crafted into brilliantly colored heraldic coats of arms.

Above Sixteenth-century stone mullions, beautifully restored in the 1930s to their original condition, with chain-opening casements and old, crown-glass panes.

THE GLAZED WINDOW

Although glass was used extensively in churches and in the homes of the rich, it remained a luxury until well into the sixteenth century. Techniques of glass production were improving; glass for windows was blown in cylinders or muffs, split along its length and allowed to flatten as it cooled. Small sections known as "quarries" were cut from the glass and were fitted together with flexible lead strips called "cames" to create a larger rectangular panel. These panels were known as "leaded lights", and they followed the diamond-shaped pattern of the latticed wood so often used in poorer buildings. Until an English act of 1579 outlawed the practice, these panels were regarded as items of furniture and traveled from house to house with their wealthy owner to be temporarily installed in each residence.

Throughout the seventeenth century, leaded lights set into wood or stone mullions remained the most popular style for windows, with only the quarries changing shape from diamond to rectangular. Occasionally these windows were fitted with a transom – a horizontal bar – which separated the window into smaller sections.

Above Thirties-style metal window for a "suntrap" house (top). Twelve-pane Regency sash window with pretty canopy and balcony (middle). Classic rose window used to dramatic effect in churches and cathedrals (bottom).

As more windows became glazed, so houses were losing their necessary ventilation, and small panes that could be opened began to appear. These were set into an iron frame, with one hinged at the side to enable it to be opened or closed as needed, thus forming the casement window. A further development was the Yorkshire sliding sash. This had a stationary pane and a horizontally sliding pane which ran along grooves in the wooden frame.

The sliding sashes were often found in cottages along with another kind of window still used today – the dormer window, which projected from the roof and allowed the occupants of the cottage to make use of the steeply pitched roof space beneath the eaves. "Eyebrow dormers" were a common feature of thatched roofs, which, as their name suggests, peeped out from under the reed or straw in a gentle curve.

Below A grand house requires a good bank of fine windows to create the right impression. They may be breathtakingly large, or they get their effect from sheer abundance: or they are heavily adorned like this one with its ornamental stonework and other architectural decoration.

Above The simple country house or cottage is designed more along practical lines. Windows tend to be small to conserve heat and will be constructed in the plainest, least expensive styles and materials. A rough and slightly shabby appearance will only serve to enhance their appeal, like the well-weathered walls and peeling paintwork of this delightful tiny window, spotted deep in the French countryside.

Above The unusual and unexpected always have the power to charm, and while this many-sided, almost round house is eye-catching, it is the extraordinary windows which give it such character and a unique appearance. The uncommon shape of the building has been fully exploited with a circular arrangement of dormers and lozenge-shaped windows, highlighted with a painted border at every angle. More conventional windows within the property produce a variety of interesting glazing patterns and the opportunity to fit painted shutters.

Sixteenth-century Trinity Hall Library in Cambridge **left above** has a much simpler, more rustic feel than Oxford's Brasenose College **below** with its Gothic-style parapets, gargoyles and other ornamental stonework decorations, although the basic design of the windows themselves is very similar. The large country house **right** relies on a well-proportioned variety of windows for its dignified and imposing style. A lavish use of windows in a great house shows that it was built in an age when they were a visible sign of wealth.

Left Wedgwood blue and white is perfectly in keeping with the style of this elegant Pennsylvania building.

Left External window treatments are often influenced by local or historical trends. This solid brick residence in the suburbs demands plain white painted woodwork to preserve its air of dignity and respectability – note the bricked-up window, with the frame retained for external symmetry.

Certain styles and locations allow liberties to be taken with stronger colors and brighter effects. The Tudor-style cottage with its striking framework of black and white will often suit a brightly painted frame, whether by the sea **right** or in the depths of the country, like this delightful thatched cottage **top right**.

Below The nineteenth-century architect, Sir John Soane, built his London home to house his collection of antiquities. His use of windows – and, more particularly, mirrors – was brilliant and original. Here we see the little domed Breakfast Room. Here we can see that hundreds of tiny mirrors are set into the edges of the dome as well as large ones at the corners. The dome itself contains an octagonal lantern-light with eight Scriptual subjects in painted glass.

There are two skylights and conventional windows, some of which open onto other parts of the house, in the room. Mirror-glass strips are set into the bookcase and flank the door on the left. The door on the right is covered with mirror-glass and reflects light from a skylight as well as a view of the rest of the room.

THE SASH WINDOW

By the eighteenth century, new developments in building techniques coupled with new ideas in architecture led to one of the greatest achievements in window design ever to be seen. The sash window, although it took its name from the French word *chassis*, meaning frame, was an innovation peculiar to Britain. These sophisticated windows, with their sliding mechanism of pulleys and weights, were in existence as early as 1670, although they became more popular in the 1700s. The true "inventor" of the sash window is impossible to trace, but among those thought responsible is the great English architect, Christopher Wren. It was certainly Wren's enthusiasm for the window and his prolific use of the style in his buildings that helped establish their popularity.

The sash window itself consisted of two sections fitted to slide vertically within a frame. Each section was attached to a cord, which ran into the jamb at each side. The cords were weighted with a "mouse" made from lead which allowed each light to slide up and down freely and remain in an open position without the need for props or pegs. Early sash windows were divided into several smaller panes by thick glazing bars. Although glass manufacturing methods had, by this time, progressed tremendously, large panes were still expensive. By the mid-eighteenth century a classic six-over-six design became the norm. The larger panes were possible with the development of crown glass, which was made by blowing molten glass into a disc up to a yard in diameter. The panes were cut from the thinner outer edge, while the thicker center (to which the blower's tube, or pontil rod, was attached) was discarded or sold cheaply. This "bull's eye" glass was widely used and today is often imitated.

The sash window combined perfectly with the light, symmetrical style of British architecture in the eighteenth century, and the fashion soon traveled to America, where twelve-pane sashes soon graced the elegant timber-clad houses of New England, replacing the old traditional casement windows.

Along with the sash window in Britain came a revival of the square-sided and half-hexagonal bay. Bay windows had fallen out of fashion when the new classical

Right The classic nineteenth-century bay window provides a little extra space indoors and affords good views both up and down the street.

Right Simple windows follow the shape of the roof in this pretty country cottage. The semi-circular fanlight above the front door is a useful device for lighting a dark hallway or landing.

styles of the mid-seventeenth century became popular, but by the mid-eighteenth century, architects were using the style to add interest to the plain-fronted country houses of the gentry. Bow windows were also introduced in this period. These windows were curved and became especially popular in the new and fashionable seaside resorts. By the end of the eighteenth century, smaller houses were adopting the styles of the great country homes and sported windows ranging from the gently curved to the fully projecting semi-circular, complete with curved sash frames and curved glass.

In place of the sash window, France, Italy and Germany made extensive use of a type of casement window in which both panes opened inward. The windows were closed and locked shut by means of an *espagnolette;* a single vertical rod which, when a central handle was turned, extended into a bracket at the top and bottom of the window frame. These windows enabled the occupants to take full advantage of the weather and also allowed them to open and close their external hinged shutters with ease.

As European colonial power spread, so the architectural styles of Europe were recreated in distant countries. Classic French windows can still be seen in New Orleans, complete with shaded balconies and slatted shutters to keep out the baking sun. In the British colonies in India, Australia and New Zealand, elegant English styles were adapted to the hot and often humid climates.

Dormer windows are built into the roof so that the attic space can be used as living quarters. With its own roof and set at the correct angle, the dormer can look highly attractive, even when installed in a building conversion **left**. Where an old building of historical charm or importance is being converted into a practical home, it helps to keep windows as unobtrusive as possible. In the Danish barn conversion **above** they are designed to resemble the original openings as closely as possible.

Right The bay window is a useful device to add extra light and space to a room without altering the external dimensions of the building. They were a favorite feature in the nineteenth century when both upper and lower story bays were popular and often highly ornamented.

Right This nineteenth-century house in Denmark has a larger-than-average window; it belonged to the artist Drachmann and was designed to flood his studio with light.

Left A strikingly designed, modern corner window gives excellent views of a Mediterranean hillside.

Below The distinctly cottage-style "eyebrow" dormer which is usually set into thatch or sometimes, as here, old-fashioned, narrow slate roof tiles.

Right A colonial-style home with ground level windows well shaded by a pretty veranda. The fine large dormer provides extra living space.

TECHNOLOGICAL ADVANCES

Techniques in glass manufacture improved during the Industrial Revolution, and huge panes of crown glass were produced, with the result that there was less need for glazing bars as windows could be made from a single pane. But the Victorian passion for all things medieval (spurred to a great degree by the new Houses of Parliament rebuilt after a fire in the 1830s) finally banished symmetry and classical styles and led to the revival of gothic architecture. Bays, oriels, stained glass panels, circular windows, fanlights and tracery were all combined to create some of the most ostentatious buildings ever seen. Mass-production made ornamentation relatively cheap, so builders added to the pattern-book styles without hesitation.

The fashion for nostalgia produced another style much favored by the Victorians which first came into being at the beginning of the century – that of the Picturesque. The many "quaint" cottages, built to imitate the homes of the true cottage dwellers may seem attractive today, but they had little in common with the tumbledown hovels in which the nineteenth-century European peasant lived. All number of features were incorporated into these buildings, and the small casement or sash windows glittered with leaded lights, heavy latticework and ornate wood and stone tracery.

In 1851, recent advances in technology went on show to all the world when Prince Albert opened the Great Exhibition of the Industry of All Nations at the Crystal Palace outside London. But it was the Crystal Palace itself that proved the great wonder of the exhibition: 1,500 ft. (461.5 m) long and covering 26 acres, it was built entirely from iron and glass and started a fashion for the conservatory or sunroom that has endured until this day.

The end of the nineteenth century saw a gradual move away from the heavily populated towns. Aided by the development of the railroads, the suburbs evolved, and soon city workers hankered after the new houses which were springing up on the outskirts. By the turn of the century, architectural styles became simpler, and the sash window gave way to the wooden casement which matched the architects' mock Tudor designs. Once again, bays and oriels were used for decorative effect, this time with leaded lights and stained glass panels to

Right Modern glass technology has enabled whole walls to be glazed, effectively lessening the distinction between indoors and outdoors, especially when the room opens directly onto a lovely patio and backyard area.

Left Wall-to-wall windows for a hi-tech interior, venetian blinds the perfect option for unobtrusive screening and a match for corrugated metal partitions and decorative details within the room itself.

Below Chic styling and easy-care options for today, but designed along traditional lines. This upper-story bay adds interest to an architect-designed home and makes an attractive feature.

imitate fifteenth-century styles. But together with these nostalgic, idealized homes came all the latest technological developments. The suntrap houses built in the 1930s utilized steel for the window frames, which were often curved for a clean, streamlined effect. New technology enabled windowpanes to grow to extraordinary proportions, finishing with the huge picture windows and patio doors of the 1950s.

WINDOWS TODAY

Today our houses display an endless range of window styles, both traditional and modern. Technology enables traditional homes to retain the appropriate style of windows without sacrificing too many of the comforts of modern living, while new designs, complete with anti-rot frames, double-glazed panes and heat-conserving glass, are incorporated into new buildings.

Traditional styles have been updated, and casement windows are still with us. They are predominantly metal-framed, available in silver-gray or anodized, color finish aluminum, galvanized or white finish steel and unplasticized polyvinyl chloride (uPVC). They generally consist of a side-opening casement, or a pair, and a smaller, top-opening pane called a vent-light. Sash windows are also available in a choice of materials and usually feature a system of spiral spring lift units instead of old-fashioned weights, which makes them much more reliable.

A more recent idea, and one which is becoming increasingly popular, is pivoting windows. These are particularly convenient on upper floors since they are safe and easy to clean: the large central pane pivots in the middle to allow easy access to the glass on both sides. Similarly, tilt and turn windows offer the best of both worlds; a window that opens from the side like a casement which can easily be swiveled and tilted, depending on which way you turn the handle. Modern houses are constructed using traditional window styles, and oriels, bays and dormers can all be seen on the most recent subdivisions. Skylights, once an endless source of leaks and drafts, fit snugly and unobtrusively into the roof space providing, like the rest of today's windows, the perfect answer to our ancestors' dreams – a weather-proof hole offering light and ventilation.

Below No treatment is necessary that might hide a single inch of this magnificent sea view; the small, square, individually opening panes offer a charm and flexibility that a large picture window never could.

Right The extended scope modern glass technology has given to the architect's imagination is amply demonstrated by the splendid dormer window.

Right Some windows should be allowed to speak for themselves. The idiosyncratic windows of this converted building need no adornment, nothing which would obscure them.

Right The floor-to-ceiling windows of this hilltop house provide another example of how modern glass has extended design possibilities. Note how choice of paint and color contribute considerably to the effect: stark white to complement sharp angles; a soft mossy green to blend with a wooded view beyond.

Right Windows ravaged by
extremes of weather in Cordoba.
Tall, curtained French doors
and exterior blinds of colored
wood give the occupants
maximum control over the
amount of light, heat and air
entering the room.

Above Peeling shutters and plain
window surrounds in a
picturesquely "unrestored"
condition in Portugal. Two slim,
arched openings side by side make
an unusual and attractive balcony
feature.

Left An unmistakably European
main street with a variety of
balcony styles and treatments
from simple railings and
ornamental wrought iron to
ancient wooden balustrades.

Below Mediterranean privacy: windows well-shuttered against the elements. The painted shutters have been bleached by the elements to the same shade as the surrounding stonework.

Above Intricate ironwork beloved by Spanish architects offers both security and ornamentation.

Right Window given the full treatment with a decorative plasterwork surround, ornamental wrought-iron railings and timber louvered shutters within.

Right Spanish version of the bay window with intricate decoration and external blinds. Other windows in the block are deep set and more simply ornamented, keeping rooms cool and shady.

Left In Skagen, Denmark, this old house was built for an artist. The fine, large window is original, letting plenty of light into the studio and giving clear views of the nearby seashore. The dark blue contrasts well with the white-painted wall, without drawing too much attention to the frame itself.

Right Original shop windows in Delft. Their size gives a clue to the affluence of the city when these shops were built. Now their slight unevenness adds to their charm.

Right A small but decorative wrought-iron balcony adorns an elaborately-framed Spanish window. A thick cloth shade partially covers it in the heat of the day.

Above Windows well-shuttered against a hot Spanish sun give no clues to the interior within. The long, thin casement window on the left echoes the shapes of the openings onto the balconies.

A closer study of a particular local architectural style reveals how windows make an important contribution to the total look and atmosphere of a region. The squat adobe buildings of New Mexico **left** have the simplest, smallest windows, installed strictly for practical reasons and with complete disregard for the magnificent mountain vista beyond. The tiny Mexican window **below**, little more than a hole in the bright blue painted wall, has been more decoratively dressed with paint, tiles, plants and a miniature curly iron balcony. The russet walls, tiny flower-filled balconies and billowing linen are an equally distinctive feature of Italy **right**.

Chapter Two

F A C A D E S

◇

MATCHING WINDOWS TO BUILDINGS

indows are undoubtedly the most important visual part of any building's exterior. Their shape and size create the character and set the style, whether the property be modern or a period design. The development of windows over the centuries has brought about a series of quite distinctive styles which are instantly recognizable and can be a more reliable means than any other architectural feature for dating a building. And so it is essential, when considering windows old and new, to think carefully about their style in relation to the building; to replace like with like, and to install the new sympathetically.

In England, it is often presumed that a bricked-up, blank or mock window is a result of a window tax which was introduced in 1695 and decreed that all houses built with more than six windows were required to pay a tax for each additional window. In many cases, this led to some rapid handy work, and all kinds of ingenious ideas were devised to evade the tax, including replacing the glass with thin sheets of lead painted white. However,

windows were sometimes blocked because of the internal reorganization of the rooms. In eighteenth-century buildings, a false or blind window was often incorporated simply to maintain the symmetry of the building. This can be identified by the fact that the infilling would be recessed or bonded into the surrounding wall, although *trompe l'oeil* windows were sometimes painted on to achieve the required illusion.

THE REPLACEMENT PROBLEM

When considering window replacement in an old building, it is always worth choosing something as close to the original design as possible. It is generally a mistake to consider enlarging the window area (which would invariably spoil the basic proportions of both the house and the room). If you are not careful you are in danger of spoiling the look or atmosphere that first drew you to the building. Should you need extra light, it may be better to consider adding an additional window in suitable style,

Previous page An example of Indian influence in Brighton with distinctly English regency overtones. This building, the Dome, took its architectural lead from the adjacent Royal Pavilion, famous for the extravagance of its onion domes and other exotic embellishments.

Right The upper story bay window was an important feature of the turn of-the-century "villa," where it offered a little extra internal space and was a fine decorative feature.

maybe on an end gable wall where it will be fairly unobtrusive or, on an upper floor, inserting skylights does minimal damage to the exterior appearance though they will only suit certain interiors. However, it is a good idea to enlist the help of a good and sympathetic architect when undertaking the restoration of any building of particular historical interest.

Where the original windows survive, it is worth exploring the possibilities of repair. Modern three-part preservative treatments, consisting of a wood hardener, filler and special tablets that can be inserted into pre-drilled holes, can work wonders with partially rotten wooden frames and are something you can do yourself. But if the damage has gone too far, you may have to replace the rotten part completely. This is fine if you have the time, inclination and know-how, but could be expensive if you have to find a professional to undertake the task. However, spare parts such as glazing bars – and sometimes spare windows – can be found in architectural salvage yards, and these are well worth a visit before you order a completely new set of windows.

If secondhand windows are out of the question, a poor condition original or a sole survivor might be useful as a pattern for newly constructed windows. Generally speaking though, successful and sensitive replacement will involve a little research; your local library should be able to supply you with a detailed reference book on historical and local styles. Alternatively, existing houses in your area, as yet untouched by restoration fever, could provide some clues. You should also be prepared for a certain amount of extra effort and expense, since the correct style of windows will rarely be standard. It may seem like a minor detail when you are making your choice, but a slightly thicker glazing bar or nine panes instead of six could make a world of difference to the total look once the windows are installed. For the purists, even the quality of the glass is important, although old-fashioned and slightly irregular crown glass is not readily available today.

LINTELS AND ARCHES

When tackling replacement work in an older property, you will often have to consider more than just the windows themselves. Sometimes, the lintel supporting the wall above the window will also need replacing, and this can be another area fraught with pitfalls if you are hoping to maintain the original appearance. Internal timber lintels often decay, causing fractures above the window opening. These can be replaced with pre-cast reinforced concrete lintels providing the original (or a faithful replica) of the external stone or timber lintel is replaced as well. If you use timber, it is important to make sure it is well seasoned to prevent any unwanted movement once it is installed. It would be a mistake to use concrete external lintels, especially if, as sometimes is sadly the case, it is mocked up with cement to simulate stone. The correct style exterior lintel or arch is essential to the general look of a period window, and there are often local or architectural patterns to consider when restoration is undertaken.

TRADITIONAL STYLE

If an older property has already received "new" windows, you will have to use your discretion and a little conscientious research to decide if and how they should be restored. For the timber-framed property, wooden mullion casements and sash windows can be carefully repaired or copied, bearing in mind the thickness of the glazing bars and the quality of the hardwood timber. Cast-iron windows were popular at the beginning of the nineteenth century, and they can often be cleaned up and treated against rust, although replacements can be hard to find if decay has gone too far. Stone-built houses often feature stone or timber mullions. Originals can often be repaired, but replacements are rarely satisfactory unless custom made. With houses built of chalk, flint, cobbles and pebbles, simple timber or stone mullioned frames are most common, incorporating casements or horizontally sliding, double-hung sashes, although cast-iron casements are sometimes found in properties dated around 1800. Typical later colonial and Victorian houses are most likely to feature double-hung sashes, although casements were occasionally used. Sometimes the windows incorporate pointed arched heads, and glazing patterns were more varied, even experimental, unlike the regular conformity of the early

Regency styles. Brick houses tend to feature windows similar to those found in stone structures.

In the nineteenth century, the Victorian passion for ornamentation led them to reintroduce stained glass into the home. In a great swing away from the elegance and light of the colonial era, those who could afford it adorned every aspect of their lives with richness and color. Windows, doors, fanlights and screens were set with exotic patterns, and hallways bathed in jewel-like pools of light. By the 1870s, even the humble row house sported its share of mass-produced glass, in imitation of the richer townhouses. Sadly, many of these beautiful windows have been destroyed in past efforts to modernize, and the only way to restore their charm is to replace the panels with similar works found in architectural salvage yards, or commission new ones from scratch. Nowadays, it is quite difficult to find a Victorian exterior with all its original features intact to give you an idea how to restore in style, but there are plenty of books and old photographs from this period, which should help when you scout around for authentic pieces.

Left Twelve pane sashes and decorative fanlights featuring cobweb, sunburst and other geometric designs, are a recognizable feature of the nineteenth-century town house.

Above Ornamental stonework frames a window with two opening lights and a fixed fanlight (top). Unusual, gothic-style cottage window painted a bright, contrasting color (middle). An ornamental metal grille looks highly decorative, but is intended primarily for security reasons (bottom).

The earliest glazed windows were stone or wood mullioned, the small panes of glass held in place by lead strips which could be arranged in a wide variety of patterns and designs **below** and **right**. Little of the original glass with its uneven but highly-polished surface survives, but the style remains in many of England's beautiful manor houses.

As glass manufacturing techniques improved, large panes and more ambitious designs became possible, and architects began to experiment with a wider range of shapes, sizes and styles **above** and **right**.

Left Here we can see the impact of windows on local architecture. With little decoration, these reflect the reassuring solidness of this hilltop town in Hungary.

Right Lindsay House in London was designed by Inigo Jones and reflects the seventeenth-century concern with proportion and taste for restrained decorative detail.

Below Stores and apartments all make use of a range of period styles to add interest to their windows. Here are mock-Tudor bay windows (some incorporated into a dormer structure), bays with three separate sash windows and bow-fronted store windows.

Right As a contrast, this Hungarian church is distinctly East European in flavor, with ornate twin towers and an ingenious system of window construction for providing ventilation.

WINDOW PANES

The configuration of panes is generally of vital importance, especially when considering a double-hung sash window. Modern reproductions frequently display a six-pane pattern which draws the eye uncomfortably toward the central glazing bar and is never a satisfactory choice. The majority of Victorian houses should have pleasing four-, eight- or twelve-pane sashes. The twelve-pane is perhaps the most attractive and was used consistently from the late seventeenth- to the mid-eighteenth-century right across North America, although the finest late eighteenth- to early nineteenth-century properties are more likely to be fitted with a sixteen-pane double-hung sash which lends itself to wider window openings. It is always advisable when replacing sash windows to stick with the style originally installed.

A decorative pattern of windowpanes or lights **left** can be essential to the character of a traditional building, so beware of replacing them with larger panes which might lose the exterior, or the rooms inside, much of their charm. Leading a porthole prevents the beamed bedroom **far left** from having too nautical a feel; the thatched cottage features a traditional diamond design that perfectly complements the old fashioned, brick infills. Space needs to be used imaginatively in a large converted building **right** where floor-to-ceiling windows are often the best option to illuminate all floors without altering the architecture of the basic shell too drastically. An open plan will also show off any good looking roof beams.

CONVERTED BUILDINGS

Replacing windows in a period house to the correct historical style is all very well, but what do you do when the building has never been used as a home? What sort of style should you choose for a converted barn, a schoolhouse or even a windmill? Some conversions are limited by local building and planning regulations which stipulate that the basic shell of the building is disturbed as little as possible by apertures and that the final effect remains as close to the building's original purpose as practicality permits.

Windows in such buildings may have to be limited to elevations that remain unobserved by the public, and painted black, dark brown or coated in red oxide to keep them fairly unobtrusive. The advice of an expert on historic buildings and a good architect is invaluable when deciding where they should go and what style they

should be. Unfortunately, the problem is a tricky one; all too often, when windows are chosen without care, a building loses its essential character. Combined with unsuitable materials in restoration, its former identity may evaporate altogether.

Farm buildings are popular structures for conversion. The majority of large barns were built in the nineteenth century of stone, brick, or wood. The original roof may have been replaced, and the number and position of windows will naturally be dictated by the internal layout of the rooms. It helps to be imaginative when planning how the rooms will be arranged. An open plan scheme, for example, means fewer windows will be necessary. Leaving part of the building open up to the roof with a galleried area is a good idea, not only to preserve one of its most distinguishing features, but also to keep the main part of the barn well lit. The best plan is to position rooms that do not need a lot of head room, such as the kitchen and guest bedrooms, on the ground floor, with the major living areas above.

Wherever possible, windows (and doors) should be inserted where an opening already exists; often, large entrances can be completely glazed to allow more light into the building without changing its external appearance too much. Usually the line of the roof should not be interrupted by any projection, so flush roof lights are preferred to dormers and, set into a dark-colored roof, they can be quite unobtrusive. Other windows should be kept as simple as possible and restricted to dark stained wood. Even period styles will look out of character if they are too grand, while painted woodwork rarely looks appropriate. Positioning a window in the gable end wall is a good way to light upstairs rooms without ruining the external appearance.

Old stables are also suitable for conversion where again, inserting simple windows in the gable end walls and glazing the original loft doors can help light the interior without the need for extensive alterations. For those who want to get back to a simpler way of life – for a couple of weeks a year at least – buying an old hunting or fishing cabin has become a popular way to acquire a delightful vacation home full of character. Many need only a few additions in the interest of comfort and convenience, rather than major remodeling work. The original cabins were often built during the last century,

and their general style and design has changed little over the years. They are usually pretty basic, intended as a base camp or rough shelter for hunters, but they are sturdily built and located in some of the most beautiful woodland in the U.S., Scandinavia and Eastern Europe. They can be left *in situ*, but they are sometimes moved, lock, stock and rain barrel, to a preferred beauty spot if a site can be purchased or leased. Their rustic charm needs little alteration, with small wooden sash windows or old-fashioned double casements their main point of architectural interest. Many will also include a big wooden front

Above The owners of this converted Victorian stable chose to incorporate windows in appropriate period style to produce an acceptable and attractive-looking home.

porch, some of which· (depending on the view and fierceness of the prevailing weather) surround three sides of the building. Living quarters tend to be rather limited, with one big room originally serving as living, cooking and dining room. Many feature an open fireplace, exposed beams and stonework, and usually a bare wooden floor. An extension is usually needed to provide bedroom and bathroom facilities: hopefully, it can be added at the back in a sympathetic style, with windows designed to match the originals, but, sadly, this is not always the case. Inside, the treatment is generally more reliable: simple, country-style furniture and furnishings, with plain gingham or floral curtains or simple wooden shutters at the windows.

A character home is often the incentive in rural areas to renovate and convert a run-down cottage, unused cabin or farm building into an attractive and practical dwelling. However, under the pressure of limited available space and the urge to find somewhere to live at reasonable cost in the city center, neglected commercial buildings in urban areas are increasingly being commandeered and transformed into spacious apartments. They have a dramatic hi-tech charm of their own which, if sensibly redesigned and finished in suitable style, can look quite stunning. Many such buildings were originally constructed at the turn of the century and are now rendered obsolete only by modern manufacturing techniques and light industry's move away from town centers. They are generally of good, solid, traditional – even atmospheric – construction. Such properties tend to come onto the market en masse, when previously run-down areas such as New York's SoHo or London's Docklands are cleaned up and sold off as homes, with a whole new status as a fashionable address. Originally intended for bulk storage or small-scale machine-tool work, their large, airy spaces tend to have oversized windows providing plenty of light and ventilation and which, together with the roof rafters and general size of the interior, are the main feature of architectural interest. Excellent light and plenty of flexible floor space have made such properties highly attractive to artists and other artisans.

It may be necessary to restore or reglaze existing windows in the style of the originals, but rarely do a totally new design or extra windows need to be considered. The usual arrangement is for each floor to be made into a separate apartment, with the top floor enjoying open ceiling construction and skylights. The location of the building is a strong influence when considering interior layout, refurbishment and window treatments: few properties in previously run-down areas enjoy a particularly attractive view, and the preferred treatment is to keep the focus of attention turned inward. The world outside can be successfully screened with Venetian blinds – an excellent way to dress a large window relatively easily. Their stylishness and wide

Below Where smaller windows are the best aesthetic option, turn them to advantage by creating a moody interior or playing them up with a dramatic curtain treatment.

choice of colors and sizes are well-suited to the hi-tech modern style of the majority of loft and warehouse interiors. For a less stark look, natural bamboo shades or fancy window shades are also popular. To keep the whole area well lit using only existing windows, the basic layout tends to be open plan. However, an open-plan layout and the huge expanse of glass make some form of insulation imperative, and the considerable cost of double glazing should be given priority when initial conversion budgets are costed.

Below A touch of bright orange paint for the outer frame and sill adds warmth and color to a simple whitewashed cottage.

Clever home owners color co-ordinate external paintwork with summer flowers: a brass bowl of geraniums for sugar-pink walls and white windows **above left**; a bright red window is highlighted behind a screen of matching roses **left**.

Care should be taken that a colored window frame suits the style and material of the building. The soft blue **above right** blends perfectly with gray stone walls – it is cheerful without being overstated in a cool, wet climate. The strong contrast of a black-and-white Tudor-style house **right** can take a brighter combination of different shades, tempered by the brown and black; brightened by the white.

Below White paint will highlight woodwork beside a color-painted wall and is often the best choice in traditional properties where you don't want to detract from a fine proportioned window or clash with red brick or a strong paint shade.

Highly decorative and beautifully balanced: the pretty procelain colors of a Cape May house **right** and San Francisco's subtle Egyptian shades **left**.

Right Bold use of color can often be the making of a traditional, simply built property. Used to highlight doors and windows in places where the light is bright or there is plenty of sunshine, the effect can look stunning, like this delightful fisherman's house in Denmark.

MODERN WINDOWS

Modern style windows have their place, too – in modern buildings. Today's architects and specifiers have been able to take full advantage of the scope and opportunities offered by new building technology and materials that require little or no maintenance. A house may appear to be built totally of glass, yet provide excellent insulation and privacy. Less dramatic perhaps, but equally attractive, are the standard choices available for new building projects. Sashes and casements come in a very wide variety of styles and sizes with every conceivable configuration of pane design. There are modern bow and bay windows; models that swivel, tilt and turn, and even top-hung windows which can be completely reversed for cleaning the glass both inside and out without disturbing blinds or curtains. Similarly, there are "H" windows which pivot from the center. Modern glazing methods mean that picture windows can offer uninterrupted enjoyment of a lovely view, or sliding patio doors provide instant access to the backyard. There are roof windows which are designed to open quickly in an emergency and glass louvers to add ventilation to a fixed window. They are made of small narrow slats of glass, usually set in a metal frame and operated by the pull of a lever. Shape, size and design are not the only options offered by modern window manufacturers. Different materials offer a choice of practical advantages over traditional and natural materials. The determining factors when choosing modern windows are looks, ease of installation and maintenance, and the material's insulation properties. Basically, the choice lies between soft and hardwood, metal and plastic.

Wood is expensive, especially if windows have been made to measure. Softwood is relatively cheap, but it needs regular painting or staining at least every five years – more if the window is sited in an exposed position. It must also be treated against rot. Hardwood frames are generally treated with a preservative stain and varnished, although they can be painted. Stains require re-application approximately every three years. Stained or painted, a wooden window is attractive and has excellent thermal properties, presenting few problems with condensation and drafts. Recent technological advances have introduced pretreated timbers which have signifi-

Below A modern dormer window designed along traditional lines. Frames constructed of modern materials are virtually maintenance free, although they can't always achieve the finesse and elegance of the originals. Easy care is important in hard-to-reach locations such as this.

Left An attractive semi-circular window for a gable end. A traditional pitched roof and decorative windows can give new architecture a more popular appeal. Integrated double glazing offers the benefits of insulation and the heat savings expected in a modern home.

cantly reduced the risk of rot, while microporous finishes allow the wood to maintain its natural humidity level and also screen out harmful ultra-violet rays from the sun.

The modern metal alternative in window design is aluminum alloy, which can be quickly and easily manufactured in square or rectangular form and incorporate all necessary channels and drainage passages. They come ready finished in a satin silver anodized or white painted finish, although colors are sometimes available. Aluminum frames do not suit every style of house, but they endure well if they are washed two to four times a year with a non-alkaline liquid detergent. Salt air and urban pollution cause deterioration if the deposits are not regularly washed away. Aluminum is ideal for double glazing, both secondary – where a second sliding pane is incorporated – and for sealed, double-glazed replacement units. However, it does not have naturally good thermal properties, but insulation and thermal breaks mean that modern systems can deliver satisfactory results.

Also available are steel windows, galvanized to prevent corrosion and weatherstripped to reduce drafts. But it is plastic windows that are heralded as being completely problem free, rivaling wood for its excellent insulation and heat retention. Constructed from uPVC, they come in square or rectangular sections, although uPVC windows can be custom-made to suit virtually any situation. White finish is standard although brown and gray are also available. They produce a very stark, bland effect visually, and the frames themselves are quite bulky in appearance. However, it is true that they are virtually maintenance free, requiring nothing more than a wipe with a mild detergent solution, and any scratches can be rubbed away with fine sandpaper.

With such flexible materials, many modern window manufacturers have begun designing "traditional style" replacement windows, combining "authentic" designs with all the advantages of draft-free double glazing. While it is true that they do conserve energy and preserve warmth, they often destroy the essential character of old houses, so no matter how tempting they may be, think carefully before replacing the old with the new.

Above New glazing techniques allow architects far greater scope to incorporate exciting window ideas in modern buildings. A complete wall of glass is now perfectly feasible, as is this buttress window which illuminates the interior and is decorative from the outside.

DOUBLE GLAZING

Below Double glazing has made huge picture windows and sliding patio doors a practical proposition for today's warm, but well-lit homes. Here the window is virtually a wall of glass: the room can enjoy excellent, uninterrupted views and instant access to the outside, yet it loses little heat. Vertical blinds screen out over-bright sunshine or close in the room at night.

Two of the greatest disadvantages of windows in dwellings are loss of heat and drafts. In earlier times, timber shutters, screens and heavy curtains were often installed in an effort to remedy the problem, but it was not until the mid-nineteenth century that the idea of double glazing was first conceived. This usually took the form of secondary glazing, mainly casement windows fitted in front of the sashes in an attempt to keep in the warmth

and conserve precious fuel. By the latter half of the nineteenth century, steel had been introduced as a frame material and the possibilities of a single, double-glazed window became highly attractive. Since the development of aluminum and uPVC, the system has become very sophisticated, and considerable research has been undertaken concerning thermal properties and appropriate use. We now know that around ten percent of our precious heat disappears through the glass, and another possible fifteen percent through gaps around the frame – considerable figures in these energy-conscious times. Accurately designed and properly fitted, double glazing can significantly reduce this heat loss.

Twentieth-century home-owners can choose between three basic types of double glazing: secondary panes where stationary sheets of glass or plastic are fitted inside the windows; secondary glazed frames which are installed in front of the existing ones; and sealed units where two glass panes are hermetically sealed together when the frame is manufactured, thus replacing the original window with the installation of only a single frame. Each method has its advantages and disadvantages depending on individual requirements and circumstances. Secondary panes, for example, can be inexpensive and easy to install, particularly when using the simplest form which consists of a thin plastic sheet and double-sided tape. This is stretched over the window frame at the onset of winter and made taut with the application of heat from a hairdryer. Slightly more sophisticated are rigid plastic sheets attached by means of a self-adhesive magnetic strip anchored to the window frame, or contained in a plastic frame which is attached to the window using clips. This method doesn't win maximum points for aesthetic appeal and is not very flexible: unless you attach the pane to an opening casement, you can't usually open the window, although you can remove the plastic panes during the summer.

Secondary sashes and casements are more substantial and generally consist of an aluminum or plastic frame with glass or plastic glazing, which is anchored in place and employs a hinged or sliding action to allow it to be opened independent of the main window. The sliding type usually operates on tracks fitted to the window reveal and slides horizontally, but vertical sliding systems are also available for sash windows. Costs vary depending on whether you install an inexpensive do-it-yourself system or employ a specialist company to do a more professional job. The most effective – and by far the most expensive – type of double glazing is the sealed unit fitted in place of the original single pane. Sealed units are unobtrusive and present no problems with condensation, unlike secondary systems; some are gas-filled or have a special coating which enables sunlight to pass through, but traps its heat inside. Units are available in a wide variety of standard sizes or can be custom made. The advantages of sealed units are many: they can transform a cold, drafty house into a cozy home; they banish condensation; and they also provide a certain amount of sound insulation, although units with a special 10mm air space should be installed for serious noise problems. The biggest drawback of sealed units is cost – installation requires complete window replacement – and they are rarely well suited to old-fashioned properties.

EXTERNAL FINISHES

The finish you choose for your windows will depend very much on the type and style of the windows you have. Modern aluminum windows are virtually maintenance free. They need only an occasional wipe and are often chosen for the fact that they need no painting or varnishing. Similarly, the stone mullioned windows of old-fashioned buildings require no special finish. However, many windows are still made from wood, which needs regular attention to protect it from the elements. Natural wooden windows can be varnished with a clear or tinted wood preservative, but old, flaking varnish should always be sanded first. Painted windows can be finished with good-quality exterior gloss, which is available in a wide variety of colors, although white is the most popular. New wooden windows can be painted with microporous paint, which allows the wood beneath to breathe naturally and can expand and contract accordingly, thus avoiding ugly cracks. Windows which have been previously painted should be rubbed down to the bare wood first; otherwise, the paint is not effective. Metal windows should be rubbed down, primed, undercoated and then finished with gloss paint. Older windows which have not been galvanized are best treated with a rust remover before priming.

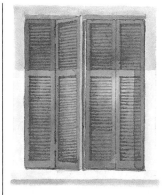

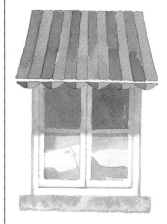

Above Mediterranean-style louvered shutters (top). A brightly colored awning provides shade and protects furnishings inside from the fading effects of strong sunshine (middle). Ocean-front window decorated with shells pressed into the cement (bottom).

Virtually anything is now within the scope of the modern architect, whether it be flush-mounted frames for sleekness **left**, or the double-glazed security of huge areas of window **above** which provide light and draft-free enjoyment of the world outside.

Left Where traditional windows were often ornate and much embellished, modern-style windows usually rely on their simplicity of shape for effect. The combination of large areas of glass with white-painted stonework, black trim and a row of exotic plants can be very exciting.

Chapter Three

D E C O R A T I V E
D E T A I L S

◇

PLANTS, BALCONIES AND AWNINGS

S ome window styles lend themselves naturally to a little extra ornamentation, be it an architectural feature such as a balcony, or more practical adornment like shutters or an awning. Such additions can transform what would otherwise be a very ordinary exterior, as well as adding an extra dimension to the home.

WINDOW SHUTTERS

External shutters can add the perfect finishing touch to certain windows. They complete the picture and complement the style of the windows themselves. In addition to their decorative function, shutters serve a practical purpose, nowhere more so than on the exposed plains of North America and Australia, which are regularly subjected to dust storms and hurricanes. In such climates, the windows of any structure form a weak point and must therefore be heavily shielded with thick wooden shutters to protect the building from the storms.

In colder regions of the world, heavy wooden shutters provide an extra layer of insulation when they are closed at night. Their style varies according to the building; they might be tall and rectangular to fit the windows of the elegant townhouses or small and square for the windows of a mountain chalet. Their solid construction and tight fit allow little light to penetrate during the day, with the exception of the rays let in by a small star, moon or other similar pattern sometimes cut into the top panels for decoration. Generally, these shutters are left plain or painted in a subtle color, but in some regions, such as Bavaria, artisan painters use traditional designs to create highly colorful decorations. Using patterns that date back centuries, they adorn the wood with flowers and animal forms which brighten up the chalets in the cold winter months. Some countries go one step further by painting *trompe l'oeil* surrounds and even complete windows on plain exterior walls.

In warmer countries, the function of shutters is not to keep the heat in, but to keep it out. Closed during the

Previous page Few sights are more beautiful than roses around the window, and this country house is a superb example with a free-flowering, old-fashioned pink variety and a deep-red rose with interesting foliage.

Right Painted shutters can make a strong contrast to a white-painted wall, and if they are matched to doors and windows, the effect can be striking.

hottest hours of the day, they keep homes shady and cool while providing the right amount of ventilation. This classic type of shutter, tall and rectangular with louvered panels, can be seen throughout the Mediterranean, the southern states of the U.S. and even the Caribbean. The blue skies and sunshine of such countries make the white or brightly colored buildings seem part of the natural landscape, and the shutters lend themselves to such vibrant colors, too. Pinks, greens, reds and blues stand out against the color-washed or weatherboarded buildings, adding considerably to their style and charm.

Such shutters, particularly in houses over 100 years old, are often miniature works of art. The faded, peeling paintwork creates a style of decaying elegance, and, while for the sake of practicality, they ought to have a coat of paint, this could seriously detract from their charm. Louvers are often individually hinged with minute pins,

each set being attached to a chain so that they can be opened or closed for light and ventilation; the iron rod that secures the shutters closed may be simple, but the small catch that fastens them back against the wall when open is often cast in a decorative shape, such as a tiny figurehead. Aesthetics aside, there are few travelers who do not enjoy flinging open the shutters of their room on the first morning in a foreign land.

Some shutters, particularly in modern buildings, take the form of an internal blind often made from slatted wood, which winds down across the window. Generally, windows fitted with this sort of blind are designed to open outward so they still offer the benefits of ventilation. This style of shutter, although perhaps not so aesthetically appealing, combines perfectly with the modern buildings in which they appear.

Right Here there is a danger that large shutters will visually overwhelm the window. A natural wood stain and a partial screen of greenery is used to play down the shutters, while the window frame has been painted a brighter color to help to give it extra impact.

Left Here the shutters have been painted to match the summer-flowering combinations in boxes and baskets. This rich purple has been perfectly co-ordinated with trailing lobelia and hot pink petunias.

Right A fine row of handsome shutters, each shaped to fit a deep, arched recess and painted to match the window frames. Pots of flowers on the sill and a decoration of deeply embedded roof tiles help to enhance the effect.

Above Split shutters like these allow part or all of the window to be covered or ventilated as required.

Above These simple wooden louvers have been left low-key so as not to detract from some fine stonework and a profusion of bright geraniums.

Left Unusual, slatted shutters protect these old, lead-pane windows in a traditional black-and-white thatched cottage. They have been painted black and white to match and add a certain co-ordinated charm.

Left Rough wooden shutters can be haphazard and quirky – perfect for this whimsical cottage in Los Angeles.

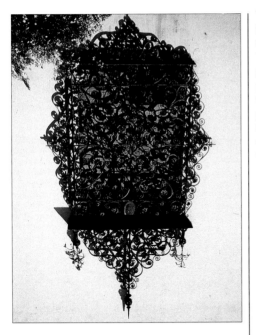

The sturdy metal grille is a familiar feature of Mediterranean windows which front the street. They can be as simple as a plain grid or extremely ornate to provide security and a possible support for climbing or trailing plants **right**. The splendid example **left** is in Seville and is so decorative it almost completely obscures the window.

In North America, external shutters are relatively unusual. Most of the older, grander buildings were built with internal wooden shutters which folded back neatly into the window jambs. These double- or triple-fold shutters were often designed to match the panelling below the window or a nearby radiator cover. Some folded across just one section of the window, more for privacy than for insulation, leaving the top or the bottom of the window exposed.

AWNINGS AND SCREENS

Another development favored in warmer countries is the awning. Used extensively in the East since early times, awnings were adapted to protect windows from the direct sun and to provide a shady place to sit on a balcony, patio or terrace. Made from a specially treated canvas, they come in bright solid colors or stripes and can be trimmed with fringes or a scalloped band. Placed above a window at the rear of a house, they rarely intrude upon the architectural style, and the scope for such awnings is endless. Designs vary, from the simple wind-down types which extend with the turn of a handle, to extremely sophisticated, electronically operated shades which unfurl at the touch of a button.

Shading from the heat is also provided by elegant screens. Buildings both old and new feature delicate ironwork panels which are fitted into the window openings to shade the interior from the sun's hot rays. Many of these screens are almost lace-like in their delicacy and, in addition to their function as a sun shade, provide ventilation, privacy and security to the home. Northern countries have their own versions of these attractive panels, taking their origins from the plain nursery bars once fitted for safety in the upper floors of eighteenth- and nineteenth-century homes. Now they are more ornate, custom-made in decorative styles to keep people out rather than in.

Left Here the awning is used purely as decoration, although this striped hood does provide a little shade to a window already decorated with matching shutters and windowbox.

Below A gaily striped awning can transform a front yard or patio into a pleasant shady place to sit and, like a kind of exterior pelmet, looks equally attractive when retracted and not in use.

Left An exterior wood pelmet has been attractively shaped and brightly painted to match the external frame.

Left Bright red awnings over individual windows make a strong and pleasing contrast to these black-and-white cottage windows.

Left An elaborate balcony running the full length of this building in Cascais, Portugal.

BALCONIES

By the simple addition of a balcony, a plain window can be extended to floor level and transformed into an outstanding architectural feature. Through the ages, balconies have been built for both decorative and practical purposes – most often, a combination of the two. The smallest are in reality no more than ledges, built to enhance the style of the building, such as the elegant wrought-iron balconies gracing the façades of English Regency and early Victorian buildings. Handmade in a glorious variety of styles, they must be well-maintained if they are to stand the ravages of time. Particularly susceptible are ironwork balconies in coastal towns, which suffer the seasonal batterings of wind and rain coupled with the ever-present salty air, which hastens deterioration.

Just as beautiful (and often just as difficult to maintain) are the carved wooden balconies, seen everywhere from American seaboard towns to the Swiss Alps. Made entirely from wood, these balconies have elabo-

Right These balconies may be small but, smothered with brightly colored plants and fitted with slatted screens, they still provide a pleasant, shady place to sit in the fresh air.

Above A large balcony can transform a plain façade and is a familiar sight in Italy and Spain. Their design and condition vary enormously from the well kept to the shabby, from the highly ornamental to the simple, yet they always remain of visual interest.

rately carved balustrades which can be painted or treated with a simple preservative, according to the style of the building. These wooden balconies, supported on joists extending from the wall, generally project further than the decorative wrought-iron variety, thus creating a miniature terrace on which to sit. They offer those without a backyard the benefits of light and fresh air, all in the privacy of the home.

Many modern apartment buildings were designed to incorporate a balcony, which had to serve as a terrace-and-backyard for city dwellers. Framing a standard door rather than an old-fashioned casement opening, they are often sided with concrete, brick or even toughened glass, which can look drab even to the most sympathetic eye.

These balconies lend themselves to a little extra orna-mentation, and the simplest and most effective way is to fill them with plants. Any plants kept on a balcony will, of course, be grown in containers, and it is a good idea to keep them as light as possible. Fiberglass tubs, urns and boxes come in both modern and traditional styles and can be filled with a light soil to keep strain on the structure to a minimum.

A balcony at nearly every upper window is as ubiquitous in a warm climate as whitewashed walls and cool narrow alleyways. They may be decorative and smothered in greenery as in this Spanish side street in Cordoba **left**; or plain but brightly painted beneath a cloudless blue sky on a Greek island **above**.

Above The balcony can be quickly and easily transformed into a riot of color using many pots of bright summer flowers. Fastening pots of flowering plants, like these multi-colored geraniums, along the top and bottom rails, makes a dense and attractive display and requires very little maintenance.

Left Balcony style can be developed into a fine art: this house in New Jersey has pulled out all the stops with balconies, verandas and awnings to both shade and decorate the windows.

Above Strings of dried chillies add to the colorful effect of potted plants on a Spanish balcony – a case of the practical becoming ornamental.

Right Even a simple iron balcony offers the opportunity to create a mini-garden or to enjoy a breath of fresh air, particularly in towns where gardens are at a premium. This block of apartments, where doors give extra ventilation, is in Spain.

CALLE DEL CLAVEL

WINDOW BOXES

Homes whose windows are simple in design with no additional decorative features can benefit from the addition of a window box. The variety of boxes available today, plus the ever-increasing range of plants and flowers, offer scope for a spectacular show of color all year round. While a simple row of salmon-pink geraniums looks perfect against whitewashed walls on a Spanish sill, grayer climes need careful planning in order to create an equally brilliant show.

With a little thought, it is possible to plan some kind of plant display throughout the year to provide an attractive view both inside and out. It is well worth the extra effort involved in planning and planting for every season to keep plants in good condition; nothing looks worse than a collection of drooping leaves and flowers. This is guaranteed to give a house or apartment a neglected, derelict air, and a good basic framework of evergreens with seasonal additions can be no trouble once established. A selection of evergreen foliage will not only provide winter interest, but also make an attractive background for bright spring and summer flowers. They need not be limited to green: the choice of colors is wide, with golds, silvers, reds, pinks and purples, as well as variegated, striped and splashed effects. Silver, white and cream are useful for adding light; they might be mixed with green as in *Ruta graveolens* "Variegata." Other useful variegated evergreens include marble-leaved *Helleborus lividus*, which produces green flowers in winter; and *Pulmonaria*, which flourishes in shade.

Yellow and gold have an equally brightening effect; dull windows may benefit from being framed in *Hedera helix* "Goldheart" or the large leaved Persian Ivy, *H. colchica* "Dentata" or scented honeysuckle *Lonicera japonica* "Aureoreticulata" with its gold-veined leaves and white flowers which turn to yellow as they age. A compact bushy plant that can be relied upon through the winter in boxes and baskets is the yellow-cream edged periwinkle, *Vinca major* "Variegata." Plants with strong red, blue or purple foliage need careful and selective use to prevent them from looking too overbearing and dominant; they are best placed to add impact or to strengthen the effect of paler shades. The strong blue *Picea mariana* "Nana" which grows into a compact ball shape, or gray-blue *Picea sylvestris* "Hybernica," would look dreadfully dull beside a mass of rich red geraniums or *Coleus blumei* with its strong reds, bronzes and purples, but makes an ideal companion to silver and gray plants.

Once an attractive and suitable permanent background of foliage has been established, seasonal flowering plants can be added to fill out the scheme. Hyacinths, daffodils, narcissi and double tulips can be forced in a cold frame or glasshouse and transferred into containers for a special early display. With flowers in window boxes more easily seen and appreciated than those blooming in the backyard, it makes sense to select the more unusual or showy hybrids so that their wonderful color and texture – and often scent, too – can be enjoyed both inside and outside the house. There are dwarf narcissi, (*Narcissus cyclamineus*) perfect for window boxes with their swept-back petals of yellow, white and gold; scented single and double early tulips growing only to around 10-12 in. (25-30cm); later flowering, multi-blooming, striped and fringed tulips; and – perhaps at their best in a window box – pink, white, purple, cream and blue hyacinths with their heady fragrance. The smaller flowering bulbs are useful for disguising the bare stems of taller plants and can be beautifully color-coordinated: tiny blue and purple grape hyacinths, *Muscari*, below white or golden narcissi; or early flowering *Crocus tomasinianus* which has silver-gray and pale lavender markings – very stylish combined with pink or purple.

Other delicate early spring flowers which will lift the spirits in a window box include the snowdrop, *Galanthus* (*G. nivalis* "Viridipacis" has attractive green tips), dog's

Right Sweet-scented wisteria with its trailing blooms can be trained both vertically and horizontally to frame a window and create a real country atmosphere.

Below A mass of greenery and bright blooms need not be restricted to country properties: this pretty combination of leafy climbers and a brilliant window-box is in a mid-city location.

Below This display of spring color shows admirable restraint: the windowbox is green and yellow, the floor-standing tub adds a splash of red and it is all set against a brilliant white background.

tooth violets (*Erythronium*) in shades of pink, white or purple; or bright blue *Scilla sibirica* "Spring Beauty." Then there is trusty jewel-colored polyanthus, which can be relied upon to bloom right through winter in a sheltered window box; pretty blue forget-me-nots (*Myosotis*) making a carpet of tiny flowers; or one of the spring-flowering heathers for a low spread of white, pink or red.

Summer is the time to be really creative with colorful flower schemes, and with new varieties offering so many different forms and colors among the free-flowering annuals, it is possible to plan fresh and exciting new schemes each year. Modern hybrids tend to be shorter and more compact than the old varieties, such as butterfly-like snapdragons, bright nasturtiums and quick growing nemesia in shades of red, bronze, orange, yellow and gold. Dwarf marigolds are an easy-to-grow favorite for window boxes all around the world and will bloom

Left Trailing varieties and a good blend of shapes and heights are essential to successful window-box combinations.

continuously with very little care right through the summer. They are perfect for the back of window boxes. To soften the edges of the container, a close-growing edging plant is required. Again the choice is wide, whatever the chosen color scheme: white alyssum – now also available in purple and lilac; *Aubrieta deltoidea*, the evergreen purple rock plant; soapwort (*Saponaria*), which has tiny pink or white flowers; the star-shaped blue flowers of *Anchusa* "Blue Angel" or quick-growing snow-in-summer (*Cerastium tomentosum*), which has attractive gray leaves and white flowers.

The majority of summer-blooming plants prefer plenty of light and a warm, sunny aspect, making it difficult to achieve a decent, healthy display on some less well-favored house walls. However, there are several species that will tolerate shadier, cooler conditions and still produce a good show of flowers. Free-flowering mimulus is particularly pretty, the blotched flowers producing orange, yellow, burgundy, brown and pink color combinations against bright green foliage. Alternatively, choose dazzling busy lizzie which can produce large glossy pink, red or orange blooms, some 2in. (5cm) across, yet remain a neat and compact plant.

Regular deadheading and replanting will keep plant displays looking good and flowering freely up to the end of their season. But without a little judicious planning, the fall and winter months – that dull and chilly gap between the last summer annuals and the first spring bulbs – can be a little empty and uninspired. Yet there

Below Geraniums are perfect for windowboxes: both flowers and foliage are colorful and interesting, and the plants will withstand strong sunshine and a certain amount of neglect.

are many beautiful fall-flowering bulbs and climbers – several of which have a lovely scent – to add extra interest to your permanent evergreen framework; *Colchicum autumnale* with large white, mauve or purple flowers; an autumn daffodil *Sternbergia lutea*; and deciduous climbers like Virginia creeper whose leaves turn such a wonderful color in the fall. For an unexpected winter display, there are tiny dwarf cyclamen – their hardiness belied by the delicate nature of the butterfly-like flowers – bright polyanthus, rich velvety pansies and winter-flowering heathers.

Some larger plant containers are especially designed to be fastened to walls or to windowsills and surrounds, both brightening the exterior and providing a fine display from inside. Window boxes can be installed below the window at any level and provide excellent scope for seasonal changes of plants and a continuous display through the year. They must be firmly anchored to the wall of the house or attached to a suitably wide and stable windowsill using wrought iron brackets; or, where the sill is narrow, supported from above by strong ties. Ideally, the box should be the same width as the sill from front to back. Wedges under the front edge are required to tilt it slightly backward. Boxes should be at least 9in. (23cm) deep to prevent the soil from drying out too quickly – a common problem with container-grown plants in exposed places. Plants can be positioned directly in the container or individual pots inserted and packed with damp peat. As with pots on balconies, soil and water can spill from the box down the vertical surface of the wall, so drainage holes are not practical. A good layer of small stones, gravel or broken china in the bottom of the container, topped with a layer of moss, then a clean, lightweight, loamless potting mixture should provide adequate drainage. Alternatively, use a drip tray beneath the box, or box liners made of plastic or metal with integral drainage holes. The beauty of liners is that a spare one can be planted and brought up to the desired point of maturity each season to maintain a continuous display. Window boxes might be tailor-made in a durable hardwood or well treated (with non-toxic preservative) softwood and painted or stained to match sill or window frame. Alternative options for window boxes include terracotta, aluminum, concrete, plastic and fiberglass.

Virginia creeper, *Parthenocissus*, will quickly cover walls, roofs, even doors and windows if you let it. It looks lovely, softening an older-style property **left**. Before the first frosts, it turns a magnificent color, and there are various varieties including this beautiful blend of rich shades, nearly obscuring an old window **right**, *P. tricuspidata "Veitchii."*

Above left A fast-growing flowering climber will quickly decorate and soften an exterior house wall and can be used to screen or frame a window. Here the window is almost obscured by a curtain of greenery.

Left Geraniums are free-flowering but hardy, and can be relied upon for a fine display most of the year. They look particularly good planted in old terracotta pots where the color of flowers and foliage can be coordinated with paintwork and other window features, like these painted shutters.

Above An attractive window has been highlighted by a beautiful display of summer flowers: red and pink geraniums in the window box and a profusion of carefully selected bedding plants below. These are plants that are quickly grown for a good display.

Right If the building itself is dramatically colored, then restraint is necessary when planning floral additions. An old-fashioned climbing rose is the perfect choice here, with scarlet shrub roses below to add a brilliant splash of color. The effect is stunning in its simplicity, yet requires virtually no maintenance.

Chapter Four

INTERIOR EFFECTS

◇

SUITING WINDOWS TO ROOMS

Architecturally and aesthetically, windows play as important a role from the interior of the building as they do from the exterior. Even at night, when they are relieved of their primary role of letting light into the room, their shape, size, position and the way they are dressed is of vital importance to the overall interior design. Windows are often the focal point in a room. By day, the eye is naturally drawn to them as a source of light, and after dark, even with blinds or curtains drawn, they remain one of the room's largest features, so it is important to dress them well, maintaining interest through an attractive fabric design, a stunning pelmet or a stylish blind.

Windows, by their very shape and style, will significantly affect the look and feel of a room, while the amount (or lack) of light they admit contributes largely to its mood and character. Tiny lead panes or larger glazing bars cast checkered patterns on the carpet, while a stained glass window washes the walls and floors with pools of color. Compare the tiny cottage casement, sending delightful rays of sunlight into dark corners, with the picture window, which floods the room with light, producing a spacious, airy effect. Both have their appeal, but how differently the room will be furnished and decorated in deference to the effect they achieve! The attic bedroom lit only by a small dormer cannot fail to be cozy; whereas a large, dominant window needs a suitably grand treatment and one that will be satisfactorily coordinated with other furnishings. If it provides a magnificent view in the bargain, that too will need to be taken into consideration.

Windows go a long way toward controlling the look and feel of an interior, but they needn't be allowed to have it all their own way. They can be played up and emphasized, or disguised almost out of existence, particularly where their function of providing light and ventilation is no longer necessary. Playing them up means turning them into a stunning focal point – using bold patterns or strong colors in your choice of fabrics, or maybe painting or staining the frame itself a bright shade

Previous page The effect of lighted windows at night combined with good external lighting: this country house is instantly warm and welcoming.

Below A beautiful pair of deep-set arched windows flanks a back door. Their elegant panelled surround and a selection of leafy green plants form a visual link between hall and garden. No other adornment is needed: blinds or curtains would only mask their architectural impact.

so that it stands out. An exciting curtain treatment can transform even the dullest window into a talking point, and you will find plenty of inspiring ideas for all shapes and styles in the next chapter. Playing them down means using fabric, paper or paint to camouflage the covering and frame, so that by day and night, they blend subtly into the background and look as unobtrusive as possible.

BARE EFFECTS

Sometimes, leaving the window completely bare, deprived of any treatment at all, can be the surprising alternative that has the most impact. The window – or perhaps the view – may be good enough to stand alone and does not need the distraction of fussy curtains, tracks and poles. It might be a large picture window or stunning expanse of glass in a modern building; or a small and crooked antique with rough timber frame, distorted glass and deep windowsill set in the rough painted wall of a country cabin. Good design or the mellow effect of centuries need no adornment, and the resulting starkness can be a real eye-catcher.

Sometimes the window is of such an awkward size and shape or is positioned in such a way that any form of window dressing is impractical anyway: if it is too close to the ceiling, for example, or where the window is too

small. In this case, it is important to maintain the frame itself and the surrounding area in good condition: natural timber stained, varnished or polished to perfection; painted frames completed with care, and windows well-fitted so that there are no ugly gaps between wall and frame. At night, a simple window shade or old-fashioned internal timber shutters in a finish to match the frame are the best options to shut out the night. They can be folded away or rolled up completely out of the way during the day, leaving the window free to speak for itself.

PAPER AND PAINT

Another way to emphasize a window is by using paint and paper creatively. The whole window wall could be painted a darker color to distinguish it from the others, with the window frame highlighted in a lighter or darker shade. Or treat the frame in a special paint finish such as marbling or stippling to make it really special. Borders are a wonderful device for attracting attention or making a feature look bigger and more important. Pretty paper borders are available by the roll to match coordinated wallpaper and fabrics in both floral and geometric styles to suit all tastes. These might be very grand: an intricate design employing several colors on a border several inches wide; or it may be as simple as a mock stencil in a single, broken color for a more subtle effect. Borders may need to be pasted and hung in the same way as wallpaper (be careful to keep the strip straight and parallel with the window frame – not the ceiling – and try not to stretch the paper when it is wet or it may not match on the opposite side). Self-adhesive borders are also available.

Even more exciting, particularly if the wall is painted, is to design and execute a painted border. It can look stunning, yet cost very little except time and patience. A simple band (or bands) in a strong color may be sufficient; or you could apply a stenciled pattern in one or more complementary shades. You can make up your own design and transfer it to manilla paper oiled with linseed oil for cutting out with a sharp scalpel; or buy ready-made stencils in a wide variety of historical and modern designs including Art Deco, Victorian and nursery styles. Bear in mind that if you are planning to work right around the window, you will need a special

Right Making the most of a modest sash window with clever use of coordinated paper, fabric and a deep decorative border. A pretty fabric pelmet and floor-to-ceiling curtains maximize its impact in a difficult off-center position. A bold vertical stripe below the dado highlights a small window seat.

corner stencil (reverse it for the opposite corner) designed to match the main stencil for a neat turn and a far more pleasing effect. A subtler, softer look can be achieved by using just the four corners bordering the window frame if you prefer.

Stencils can be applied using spray paint (mask off the window and entire surrounding area with newspaper and masking tape), or with a special stubby stencil brush. Several colors can be applied using a series of stencils or by masking out part of the design and applying each color in turn. If you are planning a multi-colored, complicated stencil, it would be sensible to use a quick-drying, water-based paint such as artist's acrylic or emulsion paint so that there is not too long a wait between coats.

Another very effective border idea using paint is to mask off the width of your desired border using masking tape, then fill in with a special broken paint effect – maybe to match the window frame, or the wall itself, but in a different shade or pattern. Paint could be rag-rolled,

Floor-to-ceiling curtains and an elaborate pelmet will make a window seem grander than it really is. It may already be large and imposing **far left** requiring this kind of setting with drapes, tassels and fringes. Or the same technique can be used to create a focal point on a half landing **left**. **Right** The extravagant Gothic plasterwork of the ceiling extends down the frames of these splendid windows and no extra treatment is necessary – or indeed possible.

sponged or stippled – all simple techniques even for an amateur decorator. To apply one of these effects, the paint is usually thinned with an appropriate thinner (depending on whether it is oil- or water-based), or scumble glaze (available from specialist decorator's suppliers), then applied to the wall using a scrunched-up piece of material, a natural sponge or a special stipple brush. The final effect could be as strong or subtle as you like – a stenciled border could even be added to the painted band for extra decoration. Any border, painted or papered, could be continued around the room at picture rail or dado level for extra impact and used to link the window with other decorative features.

ILLUSIONS OF LIGHT

Clever lighting is another way windows can be highlighted and emphasized. It may sound a strange idea – lighting a window – but a low-voltage halogen spotlight with its natural white light looks wonderful trained on attractive blinds or curtains, especially at night when they are closed. This trick looks most spectacular with grand, formal windows and elaborate curtain effects, which can suddenly come to life with the addition of a little subtle lighting: colors are enhanced, tucks and pleats are emphasized and the window becomes three-dimensional. Lights can be recessed in the ceiling and usually consist of a small swiveling "eyeball" to be trained on a special feature. Positioning lights over the window – especially low-voltage white lights which do not cast that rather warm, yellow glow – is also an excellent boost for poor natural light.

You can play more games with light and effectively double the impact of your window by hanging a mirror on the wall directly opposite. This is a particularly good trick for small rooms like bathrooms, where the optical illusion will be of a room twice the size. In other small, dark rooms, merely the light reflected can be valuable and for very little effort, produce a totally different, brighter atmosphere. The only point to watch out for here is to check exactly what the mirror will be reflecting: an unattractive window or a dull, depressing outlook will not create a cheerful effect.

In rooms which need brightening, but where there is

Above The modern window is designed to let in light rather than fresh air and is cleverly positioned where it might create an eye-catching focal point. The pyramid of panes lead the eye toward the soaring ceiling.

Left Inward-opening casements, which allow the whole window to be opened wide to enjoy the view or garden beyond, are essentially Mediterranean in origin and suit a simple decor and balmy climate.

Right An English baronial hall demands a fine entrance, and a grand window can be useful not only to light the area, but also to create the right impression. Decorated with classical pillars, arches and other embellishments, it has no need for any form of curtaining, which would only mask such a fine feature and spoil the effect.

Above A wall of glass has been allowed to dominate the room by using shiny surfaces and simple glass furniture to produce exciting reflections and a great deal of light.

Left A difficult window can sometimes prompt the most exciting effects. This splendid example needed screening, and simple net or cheesecloth gathered to the shape of the window was the ideal stylish solution, since it serves only to enhance the window's charms.

Below A simple color theme of no more than two or three strong shades will link the window to other decorative features in the room. Here the shutters and frame echo a green scheme and are a good balance for the dramatic black used as an accent color for decorative and furnishing touches.

Right Windows such as these cannot fail to attract maximum attention: circular French windows in plain varnished wood look superb in this dining room where their shape is echoed by the round table. While being wonderfully decorative, they also allow good outside views.

Never waste the wonderful advantages of a room with large windows and a sunny aspect or a fine view. Decorative lace screens loosely hung from poles filter the light **left** without spoiling the mellow yet spacious feel of the interior; stripped wooden shutters are perfect to shut out the night. The alternative is curtains that pull right back **below** — essential here to display a magnificent variety of decorative manor-house windows.

Right Where windows are as large and attractive as these, a profusion of plants can be used to create a lovely living screen and produce a leafy conservatory atmosphere.

Right Creative use of net has given a light, fresh feel to the window. Pure white drapes, clever use of tiebacks and a white painted pole have produced a highly decorative pelmet and curtain which do not detract from other furnishings in the room.

Above An otherwise dull bedroom window with an uninspiring view has been turned into a focal point with a fabric pelmet and long floral curtains swept back from the center with matching tiebacks.

Left A totally original look, and an effective means of screening the window, using antique saris.

no view or a poor one, it may be better to indulge in illusion and opt for a *trompe l'oeil* window – that is, one that is simply painted on the wall. Competently executed, and life size, first impressions can be extremely convincing, and the painted window will make as attractive and eye-catching a feature as the real thing. Another impressive and potentially exciting *trompe l'oeil* effect, especially in a bathroom with no natural light source, is to install an interesting window frame (maybe an antique frame or an elaborate arched style) glazed with obscured or stained glass with a light positioned behind to shine through.

THE ART OF DISGUISE

Making a feature of your windows is all very well, but what can be done when you don't need or want them and would rather play them down or even get rid of them completely. They might be in an awkward position and hinder your intended decorations, or perhaps they are just not very attractive and you don't want attention drawn to them. Complete removal or replacement is rarely practical – this would be an expensive solution to an essentially aesthetic problem and one almost guaranteed to ruin the exterior appearance of the building, so disguise or concealment must be the solution.

If it is only a matter of playing down a window's importance, so that it fades into the background while still serving its functional purpose, this can be done by keeping its treatment as neutral as possible, or by camouflaging it, chameleon-like, in its surroundings. Frames can be painted, not a brilliant white, but one of the softer, tinted white shades; or a pale pastel, a gray or beige designed to blend with other decorative effects in the room. A broken-paint technique like sponging or stippling is an excellent disguise when it is matched to the adjoining wall area.

Fabric for shades or curtains can be chosen to match wallpaper so that they become virtually invisible. Plain curtains are the most effective in this instance, since they can be permanently drawn slightly across the edges of the frame to conceal it and will also reduce the actual window area. The addition of a matching window shade is also a good idea here; it can be left pulled halfway down and so hide even more of the window or the view.

Once the window has been effectively neutralized, you can reduce its importance still further by careful arrangement of furniture in the room and by playing up

The setting and surround play a great part in any impact a window might have. Wall-to-wall wood panelling **left**, makes a feature of a fine pair of French doors with a matching frame. In a cottage dormer **above** a dramatic arrangement of beams and the natural shape of the roof give the window its shape and appeal. A plain but bold window shade may be all that is needed for further decoration. Alternatively, play down the window and reduce light levels with an arrangement of louvered shutters **right** which can be opened individually as required.

Below Make the most of two pairs of French doors by running a single track or pole right across and fitting floor length curtains in a fabric to match other accents in the room. At night the effect will be one of a continuous wall of fabric.

Left A casually draped arrangement of antique saris reinforces an exotically styled interior while revealing the view of lush foliage.

Above Sheer simplicity: a fine piece of furniture is the most appropriate decoration for these old timber-framed windows in a rough stone-built cottage. Leaving the windows bare only emphasizes their best features.

Below A tall, narrow window in an awkward position has been given a floor-to-ceiling treatment. The arrangement of interesting bits and pieces helps make it more of a feature.

Above Sometimes a simple treatment produces maximum impact. This tiny cottage window, little more than a squint or spyhole, needs no fussy treatment, simply a deep-set sill and a finely polished beam above, to look perfectly stunning.

Right Beautifully dressed French doors frame an equally lovely view beyond. A deep and elaborate pelmet adds glamour and emphasis to what is now the focal point of the room.

some other feature such as the fireplace or a fine piece of furniture. A stylish focal point, cleverly highlighted with spotlights and positioned to arrest attention, will easily relegate the window to second place.

IN THE DARK

Complete but temporary darkness during the day can be surprisingly difficult to achieve unless blinds and curtains are thick and well lined. Even then, light tends to escape around the edges. A combination of blinds and curtains – a coordinated window shade sitting behind and easily rolled out of sight when not in use – is one option; venetian blinds are another, but they are not to everyone's taste, particularly when used in conjunction with some of the grander curtain effects. By far the most effective method is wooden shutters which fold away to the sides when not in use. These can be solid panelled wood or louvered, left plain, varnished or painted to match the scheme of your room. The most useful are those that are divided so that the top and bottom sections can be closed individually. If well fitted, they effectively shut out the majority of light and can be stained, varnished or decorated to suit most styles of room. The only problem with these might be where an ambitious arrangement of curtains interferes, making space to fold them back a problem, but in most cases, they can always be neatly tucked behind.

SCREENING

An uninspiring view of a brick wall, or a need for privacy, may necessitate all or part of a window being completely blanked out. A large, lower pane replaced with mirror glass in a small bathroom, for example, not only preserves modesty, but also provides a useful extra feature where wall space might be limited. In any room where the whole window needs blacking out, the total glazed area can be boarded over and adorned with a suitable *trompe l'oeil* painting: the view you always wished was there or something more fanciful – an old master, perhaps, so that it looks like a framed picture.

The alternative to disguise is to hide the window from sight completely, whether permanently – in which case, you might also wish to blank out the panes to

Above Screening the lower half of the window offers privacy where a room is overlooked by neighbors or a busy thoroughfare, yet still allows the room to be well lit. The sheer or café curtain is ideal, depending on how much natural light you wish to admit, and is frequently used in kitchens where conventional curtain treatments may be impractical. This room has the perfect combination of net screening and wood shutters for use at night without any drapes to cause inconvenience or be a hazard when cooking or food preparation is under way.

Above An elegant approach for a bathroom where the emphasis is on comfort and luxury. A mellow, non-clinical atmosphere has been created by a fine antique bath, oriental rugs, framed prints and various items of free-standing furniture. Modesty is preserved by means of a decorative net hung at the window with a richly ruffled fabric pelmet above.

Below An elaborate treatment to draw attention to a small window. A deep, gathered fabric pelmet, floor-length curtains and a matching shade offer a choice of effects.

make sure no light has a chance to penetrate – or temporarily, enabling the effect to be reversed and the window brought back into service when needed. You might simply hide the window behind a large and attractive piece of furniture or a tall, folding screen. Another flexible option which will keep a room cozy as well as dim, is wall to wall curtains, lined for maximum insulation. Hung on standard curtain tracks or poles, or anchored top and bottom on wires or special tracks, they become a permanent cover-up, offering the choice of plain or pleated fabric. They can also be pulled aside, if need be, to reveal the window. An unattractive view is the most common reason for wanting to create a screen across a window, in which case you will probably want to mask the world outside without losing too much light. A permanently drawn opaque shade or curtain, of course, provides a simple solution, but there are other, more creative tricks that work equally well.

For privacy, the café curtain comes into its own, a short and usually very decorative curtain which covers only the lower half of the window. It may be ruffled and flounced, matched to dress curtains on either side and hung from a pole or rod across the center of the window. For an opaque screen that still admits a filtered light, but has a far softer, more traditional feel than uncompromising slatted venetians, there are paper or rattan shades. Paper shades are the most inexpensive choice and may be pleated, available in white, natural or a choice of colors. Of course, old-fashioned lead-pane mullioned windows did the job without the need for screens; the detailed pattern of tiny quarries provided a perfect visual baffle.

A popular alternative which immediately comes to mind, lace and glass curtains, has an equally strong, if not quite as long, pedigree and has been shrugging off its dowdy image in the latter part of the twentieth century with a wide range of exciting and attractive effects.

For windows seeking a sleeker, smarter look and a choice between complete or partial screening, venetian blinds can be very stylish. They come in a choice of slat widths – including ⅝in. (15mm) "microslats" for a much more delicate, elegant appearance. The blinds are light and easy to control and come in a huge selection of colors and finishes, from the palest pastels to bright primaries, mirrored, metallic and perforated effects, as

Left and below An ingenious and appropriately medieval treatment for an open-plan barn conversion. The large door-bay has been glazed to allow plenty of light into the open-plan area and fitted with unusual and striking screens. This system of folding, tapestry-covered shutters looks suitably rich and textured, whether open or closed, and is far more appropriate to the bare stone walls than draped curtains would have been.

well as two-tone alternated colors which in complementary pastel shades, can look superb. Traditionally used to screen large, modern windows, the new slat widths and colors mean that venetians can also be appropriate in more traditional settings, combined with conventional curtains or simple dress curtains; an excellent choice where total screening is sometimes required, or where you might wish to see out but remain unobserved yourself.

NATURAL SCREENS

Small glass shelves, mounted on brackets on each side of the window, provide a perfect surface for plants. A row of variegated ivies or cascading ferns creates a stunning natural curtain, as well as an eye-catching display of greenery. Almost any plants can be made to form a screen, as long as they are suited to their position. For example, it is not a good idea to try to grow shade-loving plants in a warm sunny window.

Although attractive, such shelves pose a problem when it comes to curtains or blinds. Unless your window is set into a recess, it will be impossible to draw anything across the depth of the shelves. In many cases, the plants should provide enough screening, but if not, such as in the case of an exposed window, the shelves can be substituted for an internal hanging basket. Positioned near, but not touching, the window, a well-tended basket of suitable screening plants will take your eye from the view outside, as well as masking the interior from prying eyes.

Alternatively, plants placed on a windowsill or in an internal window box can be encouraged to grow across the window with the aid of net or string. Sunny windows can be used as miniature glasshouses for hot-house plants, but remember that even double-glazed windows cannot provide perfect insulation, and the temperature can drop quite severely on windowsills in winter.

Above A decorative net curtain, complete with cherub and flower design, is ideal screening for a large window in a traditional-style dining room. Again painted shutters obviate the need for curtains at night.

Right Sheers or voiles are an efficient way of preserving privacy or screening an unwanted view. Equally effective, and producing a very different look, is a series of shelves or sills, useful for displaying a collection of plants, bottles or glassware. These still allow the light to filter through, but provide a fine visual distraction.

Smart and stylish, slatted wooden blinds and shutters **below** and **below right** can be left natural or painted to suit other interior decorations. They produce a wonderful filtered light, while providing excellent flexible screening.

Right Create a more intimate environment in the bedroom by reducing the window area with luxurious curtains. Here, rich red damask, caught up in the center and continued in thick folds around the walls, produces a splendid feeling of luxury and an almost Gothic atmosphere.

There are many ways a window might be screened to blot out or soften the world outside, or to maintain privacy within. One of the most effective is to hang Venetian blinds **left** which conveniently allow you to see out while obscuring the interior from sight. They are available in a choice of slat-widths and fashion colors, and can be coordinated with interesting curtain effects. Alternatively, small windows can be fitted with a decorative pattern of leaded panes and opaque or stained glass for partial screening **above**.

Above Pieces of antique lace and dried flowers are all useful for pinning up at the window as a kind of decorative screen that can be changed with the seasons or replaced when a new object suggests itself.

Above Another useful way to partly obscure a window is to arrange plants or colored glass in the form of old bottles and ornaments where they might filter the sunlight and distract the eye.

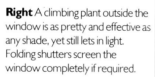

Right A climbing plant outside the window is as pretty and effective as any shade, yet still lets in light. Folding shutters screen the window completely if required.

Right The hall or landing is often the perfect position for a decorative window. A stained-glass design offers complete privacy and creates a lovely feature in an otherwise neglected area of the home. The design of this beautiful staircase window in a London townhouse makes a virtue of its shape and narrow width.

Right Traditional stained glass need not always be richly colored: this medley of grays, greens and blues creates a subtle harlequin pattern in the leading of an old, English manor-house window.

OBSCURED GLASS

If masking the world outside with screens and shutters, curtains, blinds and greenery does not suit, you can always replace the clear glass with an obscured type. Stained glass immediately comes to mind, but its strong, rich colors and the subsequent reduction in light levels do not always make it suitable for every situation. Traditional and modern designs are available and might be used most successfully for decoration or privacy in halls and landings, in a gothic-style bathroom, to fill in the panes at the top of a window, or a glazed front door or fanlight. Less dominant, but equally attractive, is decorative acid-etched glass which was once used extensively in Victorian homes. An etched design can be applied to virtually any type of glass, including laminated and toughened types, which makes it not just an attractive and practical device for windowpanes and panels, but also an ideal safety feature for conservatory glass and large sliding patio windows where there is a danger of children (or adults!) running into them. Etched glass tends to be made to order so that you can devise your own design for highly original windows, or you can choose from a standard choice of traditional motifs – either way, it is likely to be expensive. Mass-produced patterned glass is available for both small and larger areas of glazing, but it tends to be thick and clumsy with a very limited range of designs; simple opaque glass producing a plain, milky effect is often by far the best solution where you want maximum light but minimum view.

STAINED GLASS

Stained glass windows have always, since the earliest days, inspired wonder, joy and pleasure. The rich, jewel-like colors worked in spectacular and intricate patterns immediately seize the attention, whether they are used to light the aisles of a church or as a simple decorative panel in a municipal building.

True stained glass, of the sort found in ancient buildings, is colored by the addition of different metals to glass in its molten form. With experimentation, it was found that a wide variety of colors could be produced, from deep blues to rich ruby reds. To create additional

hues, the colored glass could be enameled or painted, or even coated with silver nitrate to form a choice of yellow shades from ocher to gold.

Stained glass was traditionally used in churches, and panels can be found in Europe which date as far back as the sixth century. As the Christian community of the Western world flourished, churches and cathedrals were fitted with beautiful colored windows depicting scenes which filled the congregations with awe. Sadly, much of the outstanding work created in England by the great medieval craftsmen was destroyed during the Reformation in the sixteenth century, when the Protestants stripped the Catholic Church of its wealth.

In the seventeenth and eighteenth centuries, stained glass windows were rarely incorporated into the elegantly designed buildings, whose style demanded simplicity and light, and for almost three hundred years the craft was hardly practiced. In the nineteenth century, the British Victorians finally instigated the great stained glass revival as their passion for gothic styles and all things medieval grew. By the 1860s, stained glass panels could be found in doors, fanlights, hall screens and landing windows. Much of this early Victorian stained glass is of superb quality, made using traditional methods with the finest materials. But as its popularity spread, complete streets were built with stained glass lights in windows and doors, all of them mass-produced. The Arts and Crafts movement of the 1880s saw a move away from inferior mass-production, and panels of a highly individual nature and design once again graced the homes of the well-to-do.

The latter half of the present century has seen another revival of interest, both in the restoration of existing nineteenth-century and later Art Nouveau glass, and in the commission of new works. Stained glass studios are thriving, producing both traditional and modern designs. Although technology has progressed, many of the studios employ methods of glass blowing and staining that date back to medieval times.

To create a window, a design is drawn on paper, traced and converted into individual pattern pieces for transferring to glass. Today the glass is cut using a carbide wheel, but it was originally a task of great skill, employing a heated iron to crack the glass and then a hooked instrument called a grozing iron which pared

Below The classic medieval-style, stained-glass window is a superb kaleidoscope of bright primary colors and intricate design. This imposing example casts colored patterns across the moody interior of Taymouth Castle.

down the edges. Modern glass is supplied and selected according to color, then cut and assembled. It is at this stage that any additional decoration is applied: details such as robes, faces and lettering. Firing the glass at 1,100°F (600°C) gives the colors permanence. The individual pieces can then be put together using lead strips, H-shaped in cross section, known as cames, and the whole window is waterproofed, using a special compound which is scrubbed across the surface.

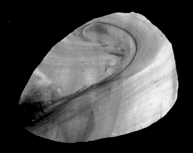

Below Many modern stained-glass artists are using the medium in a fresh and exciting way, while retaining all the richness and impact of the old by using strictly traditional methods. This design is by Peter Young.

The medieval manor house would often display its owner's wealth by means of elaborate glazed windows and expensive stained glass, frequently featuring heraldic motifs and family crests. This magnificent example **left** at Wightwick Manor in England is the focal point of a high-ceilinged panelled room. The delightful circular stained-glass window **above** is a modern interpretation, designed for a London townhouse bathroom by Jane Gray.

Above Another example of work by artist Peter Young. This time the window design has become almost completely abstract, relying on its brilliance of shape and color against a solid black background for maximum effect.

Windowsills can often provide a superb means of displaying a collection of old bottles, plants or favorite objects **above** and **right**. Where the setting is simple and rustic, the window may need no other treatment or decoration save a plain window shade, or indeed no curtains at all, to maintain impact.

Above Simple but stunning, a few plants in terracotta pots brighten this small but deeply recessed window, offering cool shade from the strong Spanish sunshine.

Above A fine Gothic-style window is complemented by a delicate collection of blue and white china, suggesting a certain sophistication. The window needs no other adornment than bunches of dried wild flowers, which have been arranged in a pitcher on the sill and hung from the wall above as a very natural looking form of partial screening.

Chapter Five

WINDOW DRESSING

CHOOSING CURTAINS AND BLINDS

T he first windows to be built into early houses were purely functional. Their only decoration consisted of nothing more than plain wooden shutters or a crude oilcloth screen, but as houses became marks of status, with the wealthy anxious to install the latest lead-paned mullion or sash window, so it became natural to use tapestry, woven hangings or curtaining as a decorative means of keeping out drafts – in much the same way they had been used to cover doorways and as partitions between rooms since the fourteenth century. As fashions for interior decorations and furnishings evolved, so too did the fashion for decorating windows, and as windows grew larger, so the scope for decoration grew ever more grand. By the eighteenth century, curtains had been refined into an elaborate and complicated fashion style: elegant swathes of silk hung from gilded rods, with embroidered wool and velvet looped back with braided tassels. Many of these exotic creations were far too complex to be pulled across the window, with the result

that one of the greatest problems encountered in grand houses was infestation from rats and mice.

The fashion for decorating windows continued into the Victorian era, and the windows of the rich were dressed with yards of ruffled and flounced lace, draped and gathered, then flanked by heavy pure silk damask. Velvet or chintz curtains were hung with fringes and swept apart by matching tie-backs. The total look was framed by an elaborate pelmet in the same fabric, again swagged, draped and tasseled. It is this plethora of effects – the different draped styles, the coordinated or matching shades and all manner of decorative accessories – that has laid down the basic styles from which we select our window treatments today.

When planning curtain treatments, it makes sense to take your lead from the shape, size and style of the window itself and from the general design and ambience of the room. If you are a traditionalist, you may want to research the exact period style and probably use fabric designs appropriate to the period – and there are plenty

F. & J. CRACE, 1841.

of traditional-style fabrics available today, many employing designs taken from the original printing blocks. However, there is nothing to stop you from indulging your own whims and preferences by dressing up a plain window with an elaborate arrangement of blinds and curtains to give it more impact, or opting for stark simplicity to show off, rather than partially disguise, a particularly fine window. A wallpaper or fabric design may be your starting point. Curtains and blinds can even be fully co-ordinated with other features in the room; matched to the curtains around a four-poster bed in true traditional style perhaps, or a modern bathroom blind co-ordinated with a shower curtain. It can be useful to pick up the design used on the window in cushions, borders and other accessories to help pull your scheme together.

PROBLEM DESIGNS

Some windows present practical problems to the interior decorator. They may be arched or awkwardly shaped, too large, too small or even sloping, as in an attic skylight.

Each has its own stylish solutions and simply requires a little extra planning and forethought to show it off to best advantage with something that looks appropriate, yet remains practical. Tiny cabin windows for example, look best with simple, short curtains – floor length only tends to emphasize a low ceiling and too many ruffles and fripperies look too fussy. Low ceilings sometimes make fitting curtains a problem, but track is often available with ceiling mountings to make fitting in tight spaces easier. Where the window is elaborately leaded, it is best to keep fabrics plain or print patterns small so that they are not competing with an already busy glazing design; the top of the curtain can be concealed behind a box pelmet or matching fabric valance. To keep curtains clear of small windows and thus maximize light, you may like to add coordinated fabric tie-backs, but make sure that they are of a simple design.

Sometimes curtains can be fitted neatly into the curve of an arched window, but this would really only be successful where the window is large enough to take the treatment. Generally, the best solution is a single floor-

to-ceiling-length curtain which can be swept back when not needed, leaving the window completely clear to be properly appreciated. Bay windows can present more problems with curves. Individual shades – whether plain or ruffled, rolled, vertical or pleated – can be fitted to each window section of an angled bay, or at regular intervals around a curved one, with little problem. Be careful to make sure that shades are made to the correct size; it may be necessary to make more than one per window, so plan the effect you want in detail at the outset. However, curtains are perfectly practical for bays, since modern plastic tracking and poles can be easily curved around corners.

At the top of the house, deeply recessed dormer windows or attic skylights present perhaps the trickiest problems facing the window dresser. Small, stationary curtains can be tucked into a dormer and held out of the way during daylight hours with wooden pegs or brass cleats attached to the sides; but it may be simpler and more attractive to design a long curtain that can be fitted to the outside of the recess and pulled across when needed. Where there is a series of dormers, the curtain might cover the whole wall when drawn, for a neater appearance; this would certainly make the room look larger, rather than breaking it up with a series of smaller curtains. Special shades are the usual solution for sloping skylights, but it is possible to fit curtains to large windows, providing they are anchored top and bottom – maybe threaded on telescopic glass curtain rods.

Picture windows can sometimes present problems, especially when, as is sometimes the case, a radiator is positioned below. In a small or simply-furnished room, blinds will often be the better option since curtains over such a large area can be expensive and their texture and pattern overpowering. But if the scale of your room and your budget can take it, curtains can look spectacular and, with careful styling, become a decorative feature.

Pivot windows, although easy to clean, are not so easy to dress, but as long as the movement of the window is not obstructed, this sort of window can generally take any style. The need for privacy is perhaps the most important consideration; one solution is to attach glass curtain rods at the top and bottom of the pane to hold a glass curtain or lace panel.

Small dormer windows can be difficult to decorate where there is often little room to attach conventional tracking, or for the curtains to be swept aside. Tie-backs go a long way toward solving this problem and produce a very pretty treatment, even when the window is an awkward shape like the one **above right** which has made clever use of trims and borders. Shutters were found to be the most practical way of shutting out the light **above left**. Decorative net has been threaded into folds and held back by a satin ribbon to add a softer, quite charming, touch.

Right Traditional can still mean minimal: a fine pair of twenty-pane windows needs only the most neutral of shades to set off a handsome collection of antique furniture; in the same way the elegant polished floor requires only a simple rug.

Left No need for curtains or blinds where foliage screens the windows both indoors and out. Note how shelving has been used to frame and deeply recess the window.

Left An ancient stone mullioned window complete with stained-glass shields and a mellow wood-panelled surround needs a suitably strong treatment in a traditional home. In this English country house, a heavyweight, tapestry-like fabric is ideal, its subtle coloring of golds, creams and dark red is combined perfectly with age-darkened hardwoods and oriental rugs. The curtains have body, texture and a feeling of luxury, but the styling has been kept simple so as not to detract from a fine window.

Right A splendid rug in shades of green, gold and russet provided the inspiration for the color scheme in this room. A richly flounced and tasseled shade combined with a flower-printed voile look just right for the size and scale of window and capture the correct period feel.

Below Floor-to-ceiling midnight-blue velvet and shiny brass make a striking and elegant frame for a delicate French window in a stable block conversion. Identical curtains have been used for a large sash window along the same wall to encourage the impression of symmetry.

Below A rich mixture of effects in a grand English manor house: curtain treatments have been kept deliberately low-key to show off a fine, brickwork frame and stained-glass infills.

Below This example of the Victorian love of pelmets, fringes and other decorative details comes from Charles Dickens's home at Broadstairs, Kent. A restrained color scheme of rich red and plain white prevents the small window from looking overwhelmed, but stays faithful to the period style.

Above These curtains at a hall window are for decorative effect only. The fabric has been pleated into the shape of the frame and allowed to hang in formal tails on each side.

PRACTICAL CHOICES

Whichever effect you choose, whether simple shades or elaborate curtains, there are certain guidelines essential to the success of the final look. For example, accurate measuring is of prime importance. Each window should be measured separately – never presume sizes are completely standard. When estimating length, sill-length curtains should fall to the bottom lip of the sill or just below, and floor-length curtains should be hemmed to around 2in. (5cm) above the floor – although it is fashionable to make them vastly over-length and to allow the fabric to billow into a froth of extra material. Never install curtains which finish at an arbitrary point somewhere between floor and sill; it always looks as though they are not long enough, or are still waiting to be hemmed.

Fabric This should be chosen wisely, not just for pattern and color, but also for weight and quality, which will affect the way in which your curtains or shades hang. The quantity of fabric used makes a big difference, too, particularly when you consider curtains and some of the flouncier shades. Curtains should use one-and-a-half times, preferably twice, the window width for a feeling of fullness; some special header tapes require even more than this to produce the correct pleating style. Skimping on fabric is a false economy. Buying generous amounts of a less expensive fabric is usually better than cutting it too fine with an expensive one. The type of fabric is important, too, as curtains and shades must be suited to their position and purpose. In heavy-duty areas such as kitchens, curtains and shades will get dirty quickly and fabrics need to be easily washable. Fabrics used for curtaining should drape well, with enough weight to hang properly, yet not so thick that they are stiff and lifeless. Nor should the pattern become lost in the folds of the finished curtains. All fabrics used for windows should be fade and shrink resistant, although a good lining, or a shade or sheer curtain behind will offer some protection from the damaging effects of sunlight.

When you buy fabric, it is of vital importance to check that the pattern is printed accurately, for any deviation from the straight weave of the material will immediately show up once the curtains are hung, and they will never look right. You can easily check this by

Below Good quality fabric hangs well and offers scope for all kinds of interesting treatments such as special headings, trims and other finishing touches.

Right Plain, heavy velvet is guaranteed to create a traditional atmosphere, especially when made up in classic style. However, care should be taken that such a weight of fabric is adequately supported and that the curtains are kept free from dust and grime.

folding back a small piece of the fabric from selvage to selvage with wrong sides together to make sure the pattern runs correctly along the fold.

When you choose fabric to make curtains, it is always worth considering linings, too. Linings make a tremendous difference to the way curtains feel and hang, as well as providing additional insulation. Special lining material can be bought and made with the curtain (which will mean the curtains have to be dry cleaned), or hung separately on the same, or on a separate special, track. For an even richer, fuller effect and the best possible insulation, thermal interlinings can also be incorporated. You will need a good strong track to cope with the combined weight of these layers, especially if your curtain fabric is also fairly heavy.

Right In this beautifully co-ordinated treatment, the choice of floral curtains was inspired by an original painting. Remember that wooden poles can be painted to suit any color scheme.

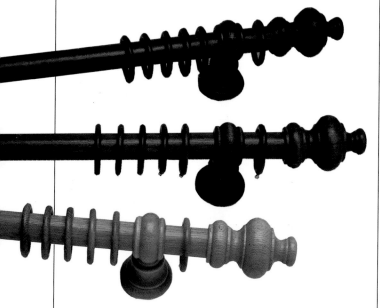

Above Poles can be purchased ready to mount, in a choice of natural wood finishes such as walnut, pine and teak.

Tapes, tracks and poles Another important contributory factor to the look and performance of curtains and shades is the header tapes which are responsible for producing the distinctive pleats and gathers at the top. There are a great many different styles and effects, some of them very sophisticated and which are worth considering in relation to the style of window.

The poles and tracks from which they hang offer a wide range of decorative options, too. These should be chosen, measured and fitted before you measure for your fabric so that you can determine the exact length and width you need. It is important to choose a fixture which will support the weight of your proposed window treatment, since tracks designed to take lightweight unlined curtains or sheers will bow under the strain of fully lined heavy damask or upholstery cotton. Poles are

available in a variety of finishes: glossy polished or plain brass, stainless steel (which can be bent to fit a bay or bow window and feature concealed runners, automatic cords and telescopic action), pine, oak, mahogany and ebony effects. Alternatively, you can buy them primed ready for painting yourself, which presents the opportunity to choose a color that may contrast or coordinate with surrounding decorations. Still more exciting would be to sponge, marble or rag-roll them if you have the patience. Poles are available in different diameters, too, so that the effect can be as light or heavy as you wish, bearing in mind again, that thin poles might not be able to take the weight of a heavy curtain effect. Wooden poles can be corded and separate corner pieces are available to slot on to the ends, enabling them to be used around corners in a bay window if necessary.

Left A strong but simple pole has been used to create an interesting, draped-fabric effect requiring minimum work for maximum impact.

Since poles are decorative in themselves, they have given rise to some interesting creative ideas: curtains need not always be hung from the conventional matching rings, nor even made up in the normal manner. The fabric could be casually draped over the pole to produce the instant effect of pelmet and dress curtains for example. If the window still needs screening at night, you will have to incorporate blinds or shutters with your more exciting and unusual effects.

Tracks Today's track designs give an even greater choice of styles and sizes and can be made of plastic or aluminum, most guaranteed free-running. There are several plastic types that can be easily curved around a bay window; with aluminum, you may have to have it molded to order. Aluminum track comes in gold or silver finish; plastic in white or a choice of colors. The plain white track is easily painted – or even papered to match your decoration scheme since the curtains actually operate from behind the track. For those keen to experiment with a variety of curtain effects at the same window, a special bracket is available which allows sheers, valance and curtains for example, to be hung from the same track. Alternatively, you can buy separate valance rods, sheers, net track, and even a special Austrian shade track which incorporates a cord lock at one end for easier control in raising and lowering the shade. With many tracks, cords provide automatic curtain pulling and for those with a passion for gadgetry, there is even a remote-controlled electronic curtain-pulling system that can be voice activated!

Below Old pattern books reveal what a wonderful wealth of trims, tassels and pelmet styles were available to home furnishers of the last century.

Trims and accessories Trims and accessories can make a tremendous difference to the finished look of a dressed window. Before selecting your curtain fabric, think carefully about the effect you want to achieve. Invisible tracks and curtain tape create a simple style, while poles, whether wooden or brass, provide a more ornamental look and can be matched to, or coordinated with, other furnishing features in the room.

Fringes and tassels, embroidered borders, lace, eyelet lace and other trimmings can dramatically alter the look of curtains, shades and pelmets. Glass curtains can benefit from a lace trim or be gathered back with satin ribbons for additional decoration in the right setting. Tie-backs, perhaps the most elegant of all curtain accessories, are used to scoop curtains into a more decorative shape and let in more light. They can be simple color-coordinated tassels looped around each curtain and fastened to the wall with solid brass hooks; or made in matching or contrasting fabric, then ruffled and trimmed or stiffened with pelmet buckram or non-woven interfacing. For a less decorative alternative, tuck the curtains back behind brass or wooden hold-backs – decorative solid knobs or whirls which again can be matched to curtain poles or other furnishings.

Left The unexpected or unusual can be both practical and delightful: this small statue makes a superb informal holdback.

Above Classic swags and tails are coordinated with wallpaper and a printed border design.

Above Attention to detail costs little in time and materials, but it can make all the difference to a stunning curtain treatment. This simple fabric rosette fastened with a large tassel highlights a beautifully headed pair of curtains caught together in the center.

Below A simple pair of curtains becomes something very special when dressed up with a ruffled-and-bound edging and a piped tie-back with a lined bow.

CURTAIN STYLE

The beauty of curtains is that they are effective and adaptable. The range of fabrics available is virtually unlimited: they can be dressed up or down with trims and accessories; adapted to a new shape and size; and they cover the window well, offering excellent insulation. Curtain styles vary according to the amount of fabric you use and the type of tape stitched to the top. A simple gathered heading requires about one-and-a-half times the width of the window in fabric and is suitable for small, plain windows. Highly decorative and extravagant pinch pleats need up to two-and-a-half times the required width. For a simple but more formal look than standard tape, pencil pleats (sometimes called regis tape), produces a tight, even band of gathers; while wide cartridge tape is particularly suitable for heavyweight fabrics and results in a larger but more evenly spaced pleat effect. Other headings include scalloped or tab-headed curtains where a series of fabric tabs or scallop effects means that the curtain can be hung directly from a pole or brass rod. Tapes are also available specially designed for use with finer fabrics such as net or lace and for hanging detachable linings.

Curtains encompass many styles and roles, offering endless scope to be imaginative and exciting. The simple café curtain, hung across the lower half of the window, is intended for privacy; but there is nothing to stop you from putting up several rows of such curtains to create an unusual tiered effect. If you gather them on standard heading tape and design them so that they can be opened in the middle, you have also created a fully adjustable system for screening and ventilation.

Dress curtains – panels of fabric too narrow to be drawn across to cover the window and purely for effect – are economical on fabric and serve a useful purpose in creating the impression of floor to ceiling curtains where you might not normally be able to afford them; or where this is not really practical because of the position of radiators, tables or desks. Flanking the window frame, they are usually combined with some type of blind or shade – either matching or coordinating – that can be pulled down over the main window.

Left The stately windows of one of England's grandest homes – Chatsworth. This rich traditional fabric and beautifully finished pelmet provide a suitably stylish treatment. Strong color and bold design are essential for windows of this size.

Left These magnificent floor-to-ceiling curtains are a practical option both for patio doors and for large floor-to-ceiling, part-opening casements. A ruched fabric pelmet with matching tail details emphasizes their height and makes a handsome feature.

DECORATIVE DETAILS

When you don't want to use a curtain pole, and the curtain heading alone isn't stylish enough, a pelmet or valance will transform even the simplest pair of curtains into a complete window treatment. Taking it a step further by using one of the grander effects, you can even turn the window into a magnificent focal point in a large room. Pelmets can be as simple as a plywood box covered in fabric or paper, and placed above the curtain rod at the top of the window. Or they can be dressed up to include scallops, pinnacles and other ornamentation according to taste. Ready-made shaped plastic pelmets are also available which can be cut to size, decorated with paint or stencils, and clipped over a standard curtain track. If you want to create your own designs, you can buy a self-adhesive stiffener with a peel-off backing paper printed with various popular pelmet styles, plus a grid for drawing your own patterns. The stiffener is covered with fabric, then attached to a plywood shelf placed centrally above the curtain track, using Velcro.

The valance can produce a less formal but fussier effect, since more fabric is used, either gathered using standard curtain heading tape, or shirred on a specially designed track. Fancier pleating styles and the addition of ruffles, fringes and trims can be used to dress it up further. Valances can also be shaped in a curve to produce an arched effect around the top of the window. Ideally, the depth of the valance should be around one-sixth the depth of the curtain drop, although a shortened form of the balloon shade can sometimes be used as an attractive alternative, mounted on the appropriate track. Swags and tails of fabric can be used to create the grandest curtain topping: a classical drape of fabric ending in crisply folded tails on each side of the window and displaying a contrasting lining.

Right Heavily lined and made in sumptuous, old gold fabric, these curtains have been allowed to cascade luxuriously onto the floor.

Below A combination of simple sill and floor-length curtains is practical but pretty for windows that open directly onto a country garden. A fresh floral fabric helps lead the eye toward the view outside.

Right This tall window demanded plenty of attention at the top to balance a high and decoratively molded ceiling. The curtains fall from a large fabric pelmet scooped into folds with matching fabric rosettes. A braid trim and matching tie-backs complete the grand effect.

Left It feels good to indulge your fantasies sometimes, and this fairy-tale playroom is brought together by a pair of rainbow drapes which are fun as well as colorful. They were inexpensively made from joined strips of solid fabric.

Above Natural materials combine well in a country setting. A rustic wooden pole and plain unbleached fabric have been draped and pinned to produce a look that is at once simple and sophisticated.

Above Shape and texture provide the contrasts in this striking modern living area where a pair of floor-to-ceiling windows has been given suitably strong treatment. A black and cream theme is reinforced with shiny black Venetian blinds for privacy and plain swathes of natural cotton fabric hooked back at the corners like giant sails. The effect is both dramatic and practical.

Right For a traditional feel, rich fabrics have been used to make a focal point of the window and to coordinate with other furnishings in the room. Dress curtains in plain burgundy-red turn the window into an eye-catching feature, yet help to dilute a busy floral pattern on curtains and upholstery.

Left A richly patterned fabric and color-coordinated shutters make a strong and successful combination, and this particular window treatment allows light to be filtered or completely shut out as required.

Right A simple but effective way to cope with a difficult, deep-set window: a casually draped length of bright fabric around a wooden pole tumbles to the floor, producing just the right note of freshness and fun.

Left Swags and tails making clever use of a bordered fabric and fully coordinated with paint and paper. The deep pelmet and matching tiebacks have made a real feature of this modest modern window.

Below For a completely different draped effect and a touch of drama, gold damask curtains have been pinned back to reveal a strong plaid lining which matches upholstery fabric.

SHADY STYLE

Where space is restricted around the window area, or where extra screening is needed with curtains, window shades can be the ideal solution. The sleeker smooth types are perfect for more modern style interiors where curtains would look out of place, but there are also softer, more romantic styles of shades with tucks, gathers and ruffles for old-fashioned tastes. Shades are also often the best option in bathrooms and kitchens, where draped lengths of fabric could get damp or dirty too quickly – or even constitute a fire risk – and for children's rooms, where little hands can be all too eager to swing or tug on a curtain. It is important to measure shades carefully before ordering or making them, since any unnecessary gap at the sides allowing light to filter through is unsightly.

Below Roman shades are the ideal option for a modern interior; they look clean and uncluttered, yet their soft fabric folds do not have the stark appearance of a plain window shade.

Originally, shades were used to protect furniture and upholstery from the ravages of sunlight and date back at least as far as the seventeenth century when window shade mechanisms were being patented. By the eighteenth century, you could buy tin plate rollers, simple sun-blinds that trussed up like today's balloon shades and the wooden slatted forerunner of our venetian blind. By the early nineteenth century, specially painted window shades showing pastoral scenes had become immensely popular both in Britain and along the eastern seaboard of the United States. Window shades were also widely available in a choice of printed cottons, silks and linens.

Today the material is more likely to be cotton or vinyl, but the simplest type of shade with its spring-loaded roller mechanism remains hugely popular. It can be fitted inside or outside the window jamb and is very economical on fabric. Ready-made window shades can be cut to fit, and kits are available enabling your own choice of fabric to be used, providing it is stiffened with the special solution supplied. Even busy patterned fabrics can look a little plain in this straight square or rectangular format, but incorporating a border (glue the two fabrics together, because stitching is too bulky) or a scalloped, maybe fringed, bottom edge opens up endless decorative possibilities for those who want a different look.

In addition to coordinated upholstery fabrics, there are specially printed shades offering a huge choice of pictures and patterns from children's cartoon characters to florals, abstracts and animals. Even the hand-painted nineteenth-century window shade survives in today's *trompe l'oeil* options, featuring views or whimsical scenes. But if a plain shade still looks a little dull for your taste, the Roman shade might suit you better. It certainly looks similar when it is extended: a plain, flat piece of fabric that fits the window recess exactly. But instead of rolling up when not in use, it folds away by means of a series of wide, horizontal pleats adding interest without taking away its simplicity. Also available in kit form, Roman shades can look very stylish in a minimalist interior, yet they are equally effective in screening a traditional bay window or combined with extravagant curtains in a matching or coordinated fabric.

Venetian blinds, with their tiny horizontal slats, are

Left Venetian blinds come in a wide choice of colors and widths. Black is popular for dramatic but business-like interiors such as these.

available in a wide choice of colors and finishes (including metallic), and are usually left down over the window as a permanent form of screening. They can be completely raised if preferred, but this leaves the window rather naked, as venetians can produce a stark, uncompromising effect. Alone, they certainly would not be well suited to a traditional interior, although there is a wooden style of the venetian blind which has a much softer, more natural look which would suit a colonial-style setting. The slats on a venetian blind rotate to shut out or filter the light and they come in a range of widths which makes a surprising difference to their overall appearance and affects the amount of light they admit. They are extremely long-lasting. Inexpensive pleated fabric or paper shades can produce a similar effect to venetians visually, but can only be raised up and down like a window shade. They are not especially durable, although the fabric types which are more expensive should last longer. A pleated shade often looks best framed by a fine pair of lightweight curtains, where careful choice of color can coordinate it perfectly with the curtain fabric. Rattan blinds have a pleasing natural finish and coordinate well with plain polished wood and other natural materials.

Vertical blinds can be equally stylish – even grand – when treated to an elaborate pelmet, but they are unmistakably modern in appearance. Offering excellent privacy and light control, they are particularly useful for

Below A flowery, ruffled shade, matched to curtains, pelmet and other accessories, produces a pretty effect and partially screens the window.

large, picture windows or sliding patio windows, since they can be drawn to right, left, or center of the window.

Austrian and balloon shades create a completely different effect. They are frothy, flouncy and more like a vertically operated curtain, as the material is pulled into exaggerated flounces as the shade is raised. The balloon shade is the more elaborate, with flounces and gathers all the way up, even when fully extended. They can be made from curtain fabric using special tape which incorporates all the gathering cords to produce the distinctive ruched effect, or they can be purchased ready made. Austrian and balloon shades are far too fussy for a modern scheme, but remain popular in traditional interiors and where they might add a softer touch, such as in a bathroom. They can be combined with matching curtains, and even a pelmet, but the effect is quite overpowering and should be reserved for larger, grander windows and rooms with the space to take it. The flounces are not easy to arrange, and the shade does not always look good at the window when viewed from outside; so, although easy and relatively inexpensive to make, they need to be chosen carefully for success. There is a less flounced type of blind which uses a similar system of tapes to the Austrian shade. It provides a rich, full effect without being too elaborate. When the cords are pulled, and the shade rises, balloons of fabric appear along the lower edge of the shade.

Left An ingenious solution to a difficult window. A ruched shade in a rich, floral fabric cleverly copes with a cloverleaf window and becomes the focal point of the bathroom, looking as good raised as it does lowered.

Below A fabric window shade coordinated with generous curtains and a gathered pelmet produces a soft, traditional impression and a flexible arrangement of window effects.

Above The Roman shade given a new look with floral fabric, fringed detail and solid brass pull.

Left A blind is sometimes useful to screen the window area where curtains are for decorative effect only, like these stylish drapes and Venetian blind.

Right The ruched and gathered shade is sometimes used as a large, elaborate kind of pelmet. It might be combined with curtains or, as here, a matching window shade with scalloped edge.

Left A Roman shade is attractive enough to be the sole form of decoration and is particularly suited to a more modern scheme, when solid or geometric fabrics can be chosen.

LACE CURTAINS

Curtain lace did not really become widespread or affordable until the eighteenth century, when a factory machine was introduced which produced a simple square mesh rather than trying to imitate the laborious manual method of lace making. This type of curtain lace has basically endured to the present day. A wide choice of patterns and designs was quickly available: large elaborate floral patterns and smaller repeats of dots, scallops, stripes and rosebuds. By the end of the century, the curtains were becoming increasingly complex and highly fashionable; some were even embroidered and appliquéd. Sometimes they were braid-trimmed and fringed, too, as in the case of window net which was produced, not in ready-to-hang panels like Nottingham lace, but in repeated patterns. Traditionally, a lace panel was hung from a separate curtain pole by a system of hooks and pins behind the main curtains. There would be a matching valance, an elaborate pelmet, and tie-backs to hold back the curtains and reveal the lace during the day. The lace might cover the whole window area, or sometimes only the lower sashes; it might itself be adorned with ribbons, bows and tie-backs. Victorian lace curtains needed regular laundering and dipping in a creamy-yellow starch to keep them in good condition. Today, original curtain lace is still available at the antique auctions and specialist shops, while modern equivalents – less delicate and easier to care for – encompass an equally wide choice of designs and options with abstract, floral and pictorial patterns.

Sheers or glass curtains can be dyed any color, as well as being available in cream or white; they can be decorated with lacy bows and ruffles, colored ribbons, swags and tails; made into panels, side and horizontal café curtains, Austrian and balloon-style shades and pelmets. The range of possibilities is virtually the same

Lace and sheers can be used in the same way as any other curtain fabric to create exciting and varied effects. Use them to devise pelmets and curtains like these, which have been swept back and held by unusual brass holdbacks **above right** and detail **above**.

as for ordinary curtains and, used in conjunction with complementary fabric effects, they can look stunning. They are easily threaded on special telescopic rods or hung from a multi-purpose curtain rail.

Visual tricks Where a window is not everything you'd hope for, or the room is not perfectly proportioned, you might like to try a few visual tricks using shades or curtains. A window can be made to look longer, wider, taller or deeper, purely through choice and position of different styles. Fastening curtains together at the top center and scooping them back with tie-backs will immediately make the window look smaller and narrower, for example, while adding a deep decorative pelmet or valance will reduce a window in height. To create the illusion of extra width, extend the pole or track beyond the window and install extra wide curtains. The same trick can be used to give height, with floor-length curtains topped by a magnificent pelmet or hung from a pole some distance above the window – it will fool the eye into thinking it sees something grand, even if the window itself is relatively modest.

Left Generous use of fabric and a talent for draping and folding will transform any window into the highpoint of your room. This bedroom has been given a truly regal touch with fully lined swags and tails, fabric rosettes and richly pleated curtains around a large bay.

Above Traditional shaped pelmet, lined in a contrasting color, and long curtains swept back with tiebacks (top). A simple and stylish Roman shade (middle). Simple, gathered fabric pelmet and colorful sill-length curtains (bottom).

GLOSSARY

◇

Annealing The technique by which glass is slow-cooled in controlled conditions, allowing the molecules within the structure to rearrange themselves without stress.

Arch Brick or stone course above a window.

Architrave A wooden or plaster molding around the sides and top of a window (or door) opening to hide the joint between the wall surface and frame.

Bay window Window with its own side walls and roof protruding from the main wall of a building and rising from ground level.

Bow window A late eighteenth- to early nineteenth-century curved window.

Broad glass see **Cylinder glass**

Bulls eye Inferior window panes incorporating the center of the blown crown glass disk from which traditional windowpanes were made.

Café curtain A short, sometimes ungathered, curtain usually suspended over the lower half of the window only, to provide privacy.

Calamanco Worsted material once used for shades.

Cames Grooved lead strips used to join small sections of glass.

Casement window Side-hinged window opening inward or outward.

Cob Mixture of clay and straw used for building purposes.

Crown glass Old-fashioned method of producing a highly polished glass in circular plates or disks.

Cullet Waste glass added to the new mix to reduce its melting temperature.

Cylinder glass Method of manufacturing glass whereby a blown cylinder is flattened into a sheet. Also known as muff glass.

Double-hung sash window see **Sash window**.

Dormer window Window with its own roofing structure and sides called cheeks, which protrudes from the slope of a roof.

Espagnolette Vertical bolt used on casement windows.

Fanlight Small fixed window above a door.

Flashings Strips of waterproof material, usually lead, to weatherproof the abutments between wall and window.

Float glass High-quality glass produced by feeding a continuous ribbon of molten glass onto a bed of molten tin.

French doors Pair of narrow, casement doors.

Gable wall Wall comprising triangular section, or gable, on a building with a sloping roof.

Glazing bars Bars dividing window sashes into smaller panes.

Grozing iron Hooked instrument once used to cut glass into shapes for making stained glass windows.

Holland Smooth, hard-wearing linen fabric.

Hood mold A projecting molding over the head of a window opening, designed to protect it from rainwater running down the wall face.

Jambs The vertical sides of a wall opening intended for a window (or door).

Keystone Central wedge-shaped stone at the top of an arch.

Lattice window Window normally glazed with diamond-shaped panes set in lead **cames**.

Lights Individual panes of glass divided by stone or wood mullions.

Lintel Stone, timber or concrete beam spanning the opening of a door, window or fireplace.

Louver 1. Wooden slats fixed or pivoted horizontally in a shutter panel. 2. Glass slats horizontally pivoting in a window.

Mansard roof Roof with two pitches, that of the lower part of the roof being steeper than that of the upper slope.

Mica Crystalline mineral which can be split into sections to form translucent sheets.

Mouse Weight to counterbalance sash window.

Mullion Vertical stone or timber strut dividing a window into sections or lights.

Oriel Projecting window at upper floor level.

Pelmet Valance or narrow stiffened fabric or wooden border over a window to conceal the track or rod.

Plate glass Glass produced by rolling out onto a casting table.

Pontil Solid rod used in the manufacture of blown glass.

Quarries Small, individual sections of glass joined with **cames** to form leaded lights.

Reveal Exterior section of a window jamb between the main wall surface and the window frame.

Saddlebar Horizontal dividing bars between window panes or lights.

Sarcanet A thin, transparent silk fabric.

Sash Glazed part of the window, usually suspended rather than hinged and generally capable of being opened.

Sash window A window composed of two vertical sliding **lights**, operated by counter-weights concealed in a boxed frame.

Silesia Thin, twilled linen, traditionally made near Hamburg.

Sill Wood, slate, stone, brick or concrete lip below the window designed to prevent rainwater from running off the window and down the wall face.

Spun glass see **Crown glass**.

Stiles Upright pieces in wooden window frame.

String course Band of projecting masonry, brick or plaster, usually at or around first floor sill level, mainly for decoration.

Tammy Strong but lightweight worsted material.

Throating Groove along the underside of a sill forming a drip for moisture running back into the wall face.

Tracery Ornamental openwork, often seen in the head of Gothic windows.

Transome Horizontal stone or timber strut dividing window into **lights**.

Valance Short curtain, often installed above the window as a **pelmet**.

Wall-plate Horizontal wooden pieces running along the top of a wall at eaves level, used to support joists.

Window board Internal sill of a window.

Yorkshire sash Horizontally sliding sash window.

Weather mold see **Hood mold**.

INDEX

ACKNOWLEDGMENTS

Quarto would like to thank the following for their help with this publication and for permission to reproduce copyright material. Every effort has been made to trace and acknowledge all copyright holders. Quarto would like to apologize if any omissions have been made.

pp.2/3: Angelo Hornak;
pp.4/5: Elizabeth Whiting Associates/ Tim Street-Porter;
pp.6/7: Bruce Low, Chloë Alexander, Nick Clark, Alfred Hansen, Erik Skänberg, Elizabeth Whiting Associates/Ann Kelley, Eric Crichton, David Mlinaric Ltd., Peter Young, Harry Smith Collection;
pp.8/9: Elizabeth Whiting Associates/ Friedhelm Thomas;
pp.10/11: Bruce Low, French Government Tourist Office, Traditional Homes/Berleigh Publishing;
pp.12/13: Traditional Homes/ Berleigh Publishing;
pp.14/15: Elizabeth Whiting Associates/Tim Street Porter, Traditional Homes/Berleigh Publishing;
pp.16/17: Bridgeman Art Library/ John Bethell, Christine Hanscombe;
pp.18/19: Elizabeth Whiting

Associates/Michael Dunne/ Karl-Dietrich Buhler, Moira Clinch, Erik Skänberg;
pp.20/21: By Courtesy of the Trustees of Sir John Soane's Museum, Elizabeth Whiting Associates/Karl-Dietrich Buhler/ Jerry Tuvvy;
pp.22/23: Traditional Homes/ Berleigh Publishing, Alfred Hansen, Elizabeth Whiting Associates/ Friedhelm Thomas, Erik Skänberg;
pp.24/25: Elizabeth Whiting Associates/Tim Street-Porter, Traditional Homes/Berleigh Publishing;
pp.26/27: Elizabeth Whiting Associates/Tim Street-Porter/ Neil Lorimer;
pp.28/29: Elizabeth Whiting Associates/Tim Street-Porter/ Rodney Hyett, Quarto Publishing;
pp.30/31: Spanish National Tourist Office, Bruce Low, Moira Clinch;
pp.32/33: Elizabeth Whiting Associates/Tim Street-Porter, Moira Clinch, Spanish National Tourist Office;
pp.34/35: Erik Skänberg, Chloë Alexander, Nick Clark;
pp.36/37: Moira Clinch, Bassetti, Caprez & Co.
pp.38/39: Angelo Hornak;
pp.40/41: Elizabeth Whiting Associates/Friedhelm Thomas, Angelo Hornak;
pp.42/43: Traditional Homes/ Berleigh Publishing;
pp.44/45: Danube Travel, Bridgeman Art Library/John Bethell;
pp.46/47: Bridgeman Art Library/ John Bethell, Danube Travel;
pp.48/49: Elizabeth Whiting Associates/Di Lewis/Friedhelm Thomas, Traditional Homes/Berleigh Publishing;
pp.50/51: Traditional Homes/ Berleigh Publishing, Christine Hanscomb;
pp.52/53: Elizabeth Whiting

Associates/Ann Kelley/Jerry Tuvvy/ Friedhelm Thomas;
pp.54/55: Elizabeth Whiting Associates/Ann Kelley, Moira Clinch, Nick Clark, Erik Skänberg;
pp.56/57: Alfred Hansen/ Erik Skänberg;
pp.58/59: Sunway U.K. Ltd;
pp.60/61: Elizabeth Whiting Associates/Peter Woloszynski/ Friedhelm Thomas;
pp.62/63: Harry Smith Collection;
pp.64/65: Elizabeth Whiting Associates/Ahn Kelley/Dennis Stone;
pp.66/67: Elizabeth Whiting Associates/Ann Kelley/Clive Helm/ Jerry Harpur; Chloë Alexander;
pp.68/69: Elizabeth Whiting Associates/Ann Kelley/ Nedra Westwater, Moira Clinch, Spanish National Tourist Office;
pp.70/71: Elizabeth Whiting Associates/Ann Kelley, Moira Clinch;
pp.72/73: Bruce Low, Spanish National Tourist Office;
pp.74/75: Spanish National Tourist Office, Moira Clinch, Nick Clark;
pp.76/77: Spanish National Tourist Office;
pp.78/79: Eric Crichton, Harry Smith Collection;
pp.80/81: Elizabeth Whiting Associates/Jerry Harpur/ Michael Crockett/ Michael Dunne;
pp.82/83: Harry Smith Collection;
pp.84/85: Nick Clark, Elizabeth Whiting Associates/Michael Dunne/ Ann Kelley/Friedhelm Thomas;
pp.86/87: Traditional Homes/ Berleigh Publishing;
pp.88/89: Christine Hanscomb, Anne White, Warner Fabrics;
pp.90/91: Christine Hanscomb, Traditional Homes/Berleigh Publishing;
pp.92/93: Elizabeth Whiting Associates/Peter Woloszynski/ Rodney Hyett, Traditional Homes/ Berleigh Publishing;
pp.94/95: Sheer Genius/Chilmark

Public Relations, Elizabeth Whiting Associates/Tim Street-Porter/Neil Lorimer, Crown Paints/Charles Barker Lyons;
pp.96/97: Christine Hanscomb;
pp.98/99: Graham & Green/Sheila Fitzjones Associates, Traditional Homes/Berleigh Publishing, Stiebel Designs/Tilbury Sandford Brysson Limited;
pp.100/101: Derwent Upholstery Ltd./Juliette Hellman & David Farquhar, Traditional Homes/ Berleigh Publishing, Crown/ Charles Barker Lyons;
pp.102/103: A. Sanderson & Sons Ltd., Graham & Green/Sheila Fitzjones Associates, Elizabeth Whiting Associates/Michael Dunne;
pp.104/105: Elizabeth Whiting Associates/Jerry Tuvvy, David Mlinaric Ltd., Christine Hanscomb;
pp.106/107: Christine Hanscomb, David Mlinaric;
pp.108/109: Elizabeth Whiting Associates/Michael Dunne;
pp.110/111: Elizabeth Whiting Associates/Spike Powell/Michael Nicholson/Andreas von Einsiedel, Y. Rees, Mereden Concept/ Kingsway;
pp.112/113: Sunway U.K. Ltd., Elizabeth Whiting Associates/ Spike Powell/Tom Leighton/ Peter Woloszynski;
pp.114/115: Traditional Homes/ Berleigh Publishing, Jane Gray;
pp.116/117: Traditional Homes/ Berleigh Publishing, Jane Gray, Peter Young;
pp.118/119: Elizabeth Whiting Associates/Spike Powell, Nick Clark;
pp.120/121: Traditional Homes/ Berleigh Publishing;
pp.122/123: Traditional Homes/ Berleigh Publishing;
pp.124/125: Elizabeth Whiting Associates/Tom Leighton/ Michael Dunne;
pp.126/127: Traditional Homes/

Berleigh Publishing, Elizabeth Whiting Associates/Michael Dunne;
pp.128/129: Traditional Homes/ Berleigh Publishing, Smallbone Interiors/Sheila Fitzjones Associates;
pp.130/131: Elizabeth Whiting Associates/Spike Powell, Christine Hanscomb;
pp.132/133: Rockingham Products Ltd./Halston P.R., Arthur Sanderson & Sons Ltd., Monkwell Fabrics/ The Publicity Group;
pp.134/135: Traditional Homes/ Berleigh Publishing, Elizabeth Whiting Associates/Jerry Tuvvy/ Michael Crockett, Today Interiors Limited;
pp.136/137: Traditional Homes/ Berleigh Publishing, Smallbone Interiors/ Sheila Fitzjones;
pp.138/139: Monkwell Fabrics/The Publicity Group, Elizabeth Whiting Associates/Michael Dunne;
pp.140/141: Elizabeth Whiting Associates/Di Lewis/ Tim Street-Porter, Traditional Homes/Berleigh Publishing;
pp.142/143: Elizabeth Whiting Associates/Michael Dunne, Arthur Sanderson & Sons Ltd.;
pp.144/145: Arthur Sanderson & Sons Ltd., Swish/Welbeck Communications;
pp.146/147: Warner Fabrics, Derwent Upholstery Ltd./ Juliette Hellman & David Farquhar;
pp.148/149: Elizabeth Whiting Associates/Friedhelm Thomas/ Michael Dunne;
pp.150/151: Y. Rees/Mereden Concept/Kingsway P.R., Christine Hanscomb, Sunway (U.K.) Ltd., Sanderson, Osborne & Little;
pp.152/153: Swish-Welbeck Communications, Elizabeth Whiting Associates/Spike Powell, Traditional Homes/Berleigh Publishing;
pp.154/155: Christine Hanscomb, Smallbone Interiors/Sheila Fitzjones Associates.